Healing Your Boundaries
Finding Peace Again

By

Evette Rose

Copyright © 2016 Evette Rose

All rights reserved.

ISBN-13: 978-1541301344
ISBN-10: 154130134X

Heal your boundaries and take your healing journey to a whole new level!! I also designed an Online Healing Course for Healing Your Boundaries, Finding Peace Again where you will not only just read and learn about boundaries I will also guide you through powerful healing meditations designed for the content and concepts that I discuss. During these videos, I will walk you through the majority of the exercises and guide you through healing meditations that will help you to resolve these blocks and challenges in your life.

You can find the course at:

www.findingpeaceagain.com

Also by Evette Rose

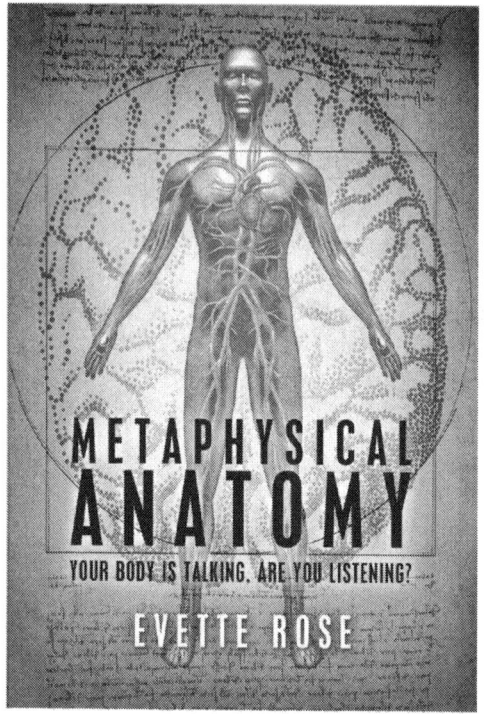

Metaphysical Anatomy Volume 1

Metaphysical Anatomy includes step-by-step guide for identifying the psychosomatic pattern related to 679 medical conditions. These conditions can be activated by circumstances in your present life, your ancestry, conception, womb, birth trauma, childhood or adult life this book compliments Volume 2!

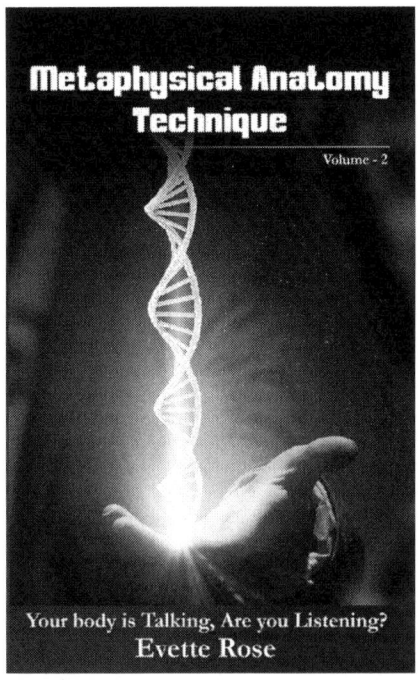

Metaphysical Anatomy Technique Volume 2 explains the core foundation and healing technique behind Metaphysical Anatomy Volume 1 which describes step-by-step guide for identifying the psychosomatic pattern related to 679 medical conditions. These conditions can be activated by circumstances in your present life, your ancestry, conception, womb, birth trauma, childhood or adult life. Volume 2 teaches you the foundation of Volume 1 including a powerful healing technique. There is also an Online Healing Course that you can combine with Volume 1 and Volume 2!

This true life story is a must-read for people who have either experienced abuse or care about someone else who may be trapped in processing their childhood experiences. This book brings an empowering message of hope, healing and understanding to anyone who feels challenged by their past..

ACKNOWLEDGMENTS

Thank you to each and every client or student that I have met. I would not have been able to write this book without you!

Thank you also to each and every person that tested my boundaries! You were my greatest teachers. My experiences with you pushed me to delve deep into my life, my values and who I am and have become as a person. In one way or another you showed me how to value, love and respect myself on a whole new level!

With Love,

Evette Rose

Table of Contents

Chapter 1 1
  What Are Boundaries? 1
  Importance of Boundaries 4

Chapter 2 17
  Associations with boundaries 17
  Using anger to set boundaries 20
  Using manipulation to set boundaries 23
  Using abuse to set boundaries 25
  Using pressure to set boundaries 26
  Using Peace To Set a Boundary - The Unhealthy Approach 31
  Using ultimatums to sets boundaries 38

Chapter 3 45
  Having boundaries with yourself 45
  Defining Your Boundaries, One Step Further 56
  Communicating Boundaries 57

Chapter 4 64
  When to say yes and when to say no 64
  Saying yes all the time 64
  Saying No 70
  Testing the waters with boundaries: 80

Giving and receiving **83**
Exercise To Establish If What You Do For Others Gives You Joy or Brings On Resentment **86**

Chapter 5 .... **93**
Setting Boundaries and Healing Boundaries – Final Recap **93**
   Are you using old pain and trauma to establish your boundaries? 94
   My own experiences with learning boundaries... **99**

Chapter 6 ....**105**
Dating for all the right reasons versus dating for all the wrong reasons........................... **105**
True love versus friendship **112**

Chapter 7 ....**131**
Boundaries in marriage **131**
Leaving the 95 percent for the 5 percent. **133**
Communicating Your Boundaries.......... **135**
Completing versus Complementing Each Other **136**
What if your relationship is falling apart? **140**
Common actions that can be the beginning of a potentially challenging problem **142**

Establishing Boundaries in a Marriage .. **145**

Chapter 8 ....**150**
   Boundaries with kids.............................. **150**

About the Author..**166**

Chapter 1

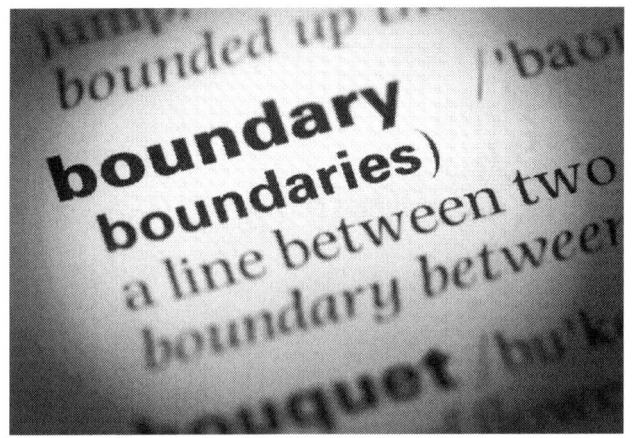

What Are Boundaries?

Boundaries are such an important aspect to our lives. If we didn't have boundaries with ourselves, within organizations, schools and so forth, then I am sure you can image that the outcome would be disastrous! There would be chaos, no structure, discipline and no order. Boundaries are not just important in society; they are incredibly important to exercise in our own personal lives. As your boundaries define who you are, what you become and ultimately how you allow people to treat you. Boundaries are something that we establish in our daily life, whether in our physical environment, with family, friends and in relationships. Most of us have different definitions of what a boundary is.

Let's start by defining what boundaries are so we are all on the same page, since we often have different meanings for certain words and actions.

Boundaries define a person's territory – the space in which they feel safe. Physical boundaries define the physical territory – where a person ends and where another person (or the outside world) begins. This also includes overstepping/disrespecting someone else's physical boundaries or physically touching a person in a way that could make the other party feel uncomfortable without their permission. Emotional boundaries define one's emotional space. A similar principle applies to spiritual, financial, psychic and intellectual boundaries and territory.

Boundaries are experienced from a very early age, even before birth! Look at the sperm and the egg, where there is already a consciousness and awareness of physical boundaries. During conception, the sperm cells move toward the egg, and they bump against the uterus wall in search of the egg. When the sperm hits a wall, it knows to keep moving and not stop until it reaches its destination – the wall is there as a physical boundary indicating to the sperm that it is moving in the wrong direction. The sperm keeps moving, directed by these physical boundaries until it finds the egg. The sperm is aware of the physical boundaries around it. The egg also has an awareness when the sperm cells arrive, since they release hormones and chemicals that indicate to the egg they are ready to fertilize it.

Even an underdeveloped fetus has an awareness of boundaries. A study once showed a fetus about to be aborted actually physically try to move away from the instrument that was about to abort it. The fetus knew its physical boundaries and personal space has been invaded and overstepped. A baby in a mother's womb also already has a sense of boundaries to a degree, by perhaps kicking too much when it feels discomfort or when the mother is doing something that is perhaps causing an unpleasant feeling for the baby. The baby can react in one way or another to indicate to the mother that a boundary feels activated and irritated.

When we are born, our boundaries start to develop even more and we become more aware of our physical environment, sensing the presence of our mother or her absence. As we develop, our boundaries start to mature emotionally and physically.

Importance of Boundaries

We have emotional and physical boundaries in our everyday life. Physical boundaries are the lines or spaces determining the limits of a personal area. We set physical boundaries in our life all the time – we build a fence around our house; we have our own little office space, desk or cubicle; at the gym we have our own locker to put our belongings in. This is our way of saying, "This is my space, please respect it," or "These are my belongings, please do not take them."

Children start to explore their boundaries and their physical sense of boundaries when they build tree houses or a fort under the dinner table. They can decide who is allowed to enter their space and who is not – this is a great way for them to explore boundaries!

Emotional boundaries can be harder to define. These boundaries are limits we project to others and they are our way of protecting ourselves. They allow us to indicate to others what we consider acceptable and what not. When your emotional boundary is crossed, you will either feel angry, disrespected or disempowered because your boundary was not valued by others.

Boundaries are our way of establishing what is important to us and what is not. Boundaries also serve as a way and form of establishing our personal space, such as what makes us feel comfortable and what makes us feel uncomfortable. Boundaries also assist in the process of having our needs met and help us achieve what we want and need – whether in relationships, business, friendships and even with ourselves.

Boundary issues are one of the major causes of abuse and arguing. If a person has strong and clear boundaries, it is unlikely that they have had plenty of encounters with bullies, abusive, controlling or invasive people. The more unclear our boundaries are, the more unclear our relationship with ourselves and others will become. Unclear boundaries are a recipe for problems, arguments, being taken advantage of and falling victim to even abusive and one-sided relationships. It is very important to understand that having boundaries does not mean that you are a selfish person; it only means that you love yourself enough to know and recognize where your emotional and physical limits are. These boundary limits will indicate to you and others what you will, can and will not tolerate in relationships, business relations, friendships and family. Boundaries serve as a verbal and non-verbal guide line for how you would like to be treated and respected. If anyone ever tells you that you are selfish for establishing a reasonable boundary, I would question that person's intention for saying it in the first place – it could be an indication of manipulation.

By not standing up for our boundaries, we are not standing up for ourselves. Building a relationship with yourself does not just involve self-love, self-care and self-respect; it also involves having healthy personal boundaries. If you don't have healthy boundaries or even know what your personal boundaries are, then how will other people even recognize them? How will other people respect you, since there are no clear guidelines in terms of what you will tolerate and not tolerate? Boundaries are not just shown through body language, but through verbal communication. If you have trouble communicating yourself, you are guaranteed to have poor personal boundaries.

Having poor personal boundaries causes a big ripple effect that usually does not have a good ending. If there is no clear line as to where and how far you can be pushed, the odds of people disrespecting you are far greater. One of the hardest challenges you might face is not even knowing yourself well enough to know your boundaries – where your threshold and limit is.

Normally when you get angry or feel resentful, yes, perhaps a boundary has been overstepped. But the anger and resentment is a delayed response which indicates that your boundary was actually crossed a long time ago. It means you missed the fine line was overstepped, and you didn't take action quickly enough in order to avoid the boundary failure you experienced.

That feeling could be, for example, that you feel you are not allowed to have the physical or emotional space you really need. You are not able to speak your truth and voice your emotions when you feel uncomfortable or disrespected – the list can go on and on (which we will get to later in this book).

Boundaries are not just emotional. You also have physical boundaries; this can include someone standing physically too close to you, or being hit or physically abused. Anything done physically with the intent to harm or humiliate you without your consent is an overstepped physical boundary. When that boundary has been overstepped, it's important to always explore why. Why did you fail to express a boundary? Was it because it kept you safe? Meaning, you felt safer to not express a boundary in the first place out of fear for the other person's reaction? Were you trying to keep the peace?

It always begs the question: How high is your level of alertness, awareness and sensitivity to when your boundary is being overstepped?

"You cannot always control what goes on outside. But you can always control what goes on inside."

- Wayne Dyer

There is a reason why you have poor boundaries. There is trauma and fears holding and locking this debilitating pattern in place. The root cause of why you have poor personal boundaries can be different than what it is for me or someone else; however, this book **and** the *Online Healing Course for Healing Your Boundaries, Finding Peace Again* is designed to help everyone. You will not only be guided through powerful insightful exercises; you will also go through powerful healing meditations designed for the each of the chapters to help you to resolve these blocks and challenges in your life!

Moving back to our physical boundaries. Your personal space is normally one meter around your body. The moment someone steps inside of this space, your body instinctively feels that its safe space has either been invaded, overstepped or disrespected. How you emotionally respond to that depends on your genetic predisposition and life experiences with physical and personal boundaries.

How you react to your boundaries being overstepped will be a big indicator of the root causes of your poor boundaries. If you do nothing and try to keep the peace, then being a peacekeeper is perhaps what kept you safe in the past, as boundaries and self-expression were perhaps not tolerated. If you react with aggression, it's an overcompensation for boundaries that were overstepped in the past and you have reached your emotional or even physical limit in terms of how much you can tolerate – you are oversensitive to your boundaries, such as personal space and territory being invaded and overstepped. In some cases, where abuse was evident, this can be a result of PSTD, Post Traumatic Stress Disorder.

You should be able to say no without feeling guilty or manipulated. You will find that the more you resist expressing boundaries, the more you will find yourself in circumstances which reinforce the fear of setting boundaries – especially since you are not taking action to stop the cycle and pattern.

Quite often, you will cross paths with someone who has an invasive nature/personality. This person may find it challenging to recognize other people's boundaries, and often fail to respect them. In most cases, they deliberately don't respect your boundaries since they are looking for someone to take advantage of. What makes this dynamic challenging is that even the abuser has poor personal boundaries; they feel the need to use anger, aggression, abuse and manipulation to be heard and get their way.

You might feel that your boundaries in life may

have been violated or disrespected to such an extent that you do not know what your own boundaries are or should be. When you finally want to express a boundary because you have reached your threshold, a big fear surfaces. It's a fear that we are all too familiar with: a fear of rejection, confrontation, abuse or abandonment.

I have observed clients who consistently failed to recognize other's boundaries. Some came from a background where they were not educated about boundaries by their parents. In other cases, the parents had no consideration for other peoples' boundaries – so their child's own boundaries had been violated and disrespected to such an extent that they did not know what their own boundaries should be, and even copied their parents' poor behaviors.

Your experiences in life help you form a general basis of emotional and physical boundaries. Painful or unpleasant feedback may lead you to avoid moving beyond certain boundaries. Positive feedback stimulates a person to explore that boundary more. People are continuously forming and reforming their boundaries based on their life experiences and the sensory messages associated with those encounters. Positive ongoing experiences reinforce healthy boundaries.

Infants do not have boundaries until they are taught. The way boundaries are introduced sets the foundation for their understanding of boundaries. As a child, there is no awareness as to whether a boundary is good or bad.

Shame and boundaries often go hand in hand. A mother might be upset or angered by the child's behavior. She might use manipulation and shame by saying how bad the child is for doing ___. The child then feels ashamed for what they have done or expressed.

When a child experiences hostility or abuse from a caregiver, it may make them feel that there is no safe place (no buffer) between themselves and the world.

I once saw a client who told me that she had good boundaries, since she yelled at her father when he disrespected her boundaries. But she needed to yell and stamp her feet in order to be heard. She did not express boundaries in a confident manner. She expressed her boundaries from a place of fear and she only felt heard and safe when she yelled. I quickly learned that her mother also expressed her boundaries toward the father in the same manner. Poor personal boundaries are not always an end result of abuse, but also what we copy from people in our immediate environment.

In my research, I have even come to learn that some people have found their sense of self, boundaries and limits through a challenging illness. They found it much easier to express boundaries when they were sick. They found that in a weakened state, their loved ones respected their wishes more often. However, the more they expressed boundaries and had positive reactions, the more they started to feel comfortable having boundaries again. Once they healed from the illness, their boundaries were also much healthier since they had no choice other than to voice their needs and boundaries.

Your personal boundaries can also be influenced by past trauma. If you were punished in the past for saying no, this may affect whether or not you feel worthy and safe of saying no in your adult life. Instead of exercising and establishing healthy boundaries, people draw their power and boundaries from anger, or they retreat and become invisible.

Boundaries can be established with firmness, yet also with love. If you were disciplined in an aggressive way during your childhood, it could set a pattern for how you deal with your own boundaries and how you express them. The good news is that you can change how you express your boundaries. You can control how others treat you by expressing your boundaries. The first step is to be clear about what your boundaries are. Where is your threshold, what will you accept and what will you not accept? Remember, by the time you feel resentful toward someone, it means that your boundaries have been long overstepped.

Define what your boundaries are. What will you accept and what will you not accept? Most important of all is to respect yourself enough to stick to your boundaries.

Now, coming back to: How you react to your boundaries being overstepped will be a big indicator of the root causes of your poor boundaries. One aspect stems from how you were able to set boundaries during your childhood, and the other aspect is the genetic predisposition of how well you are able to express your boundaries and also HOW you express your boundaries.

Remember that you are an expression of your ancestry and parents – I mean, think about it, where did your genes come from? Your hair color, your eye color – certain characteristics you already showed as a baby before you had the intellectual ability to analyze and respond accordingly to your environment. If you are still not convinced, watch the *BBC documentary Ghost In Your Genes on YouTube.*

Your ability to express your boundaries are not just based on how freely you were able to express yourself and your limits, but how you also observed your parents expressing their boundaries while you grew up. Did they use anger to assert themselves, or was someone a peacekeeper who didn't express boundaries for the sake of keeping the peace?

Boundaries and communication go hand in hand. Without communication, it's hard to express anything, including boundaries. You can express boundaries with body language as well; however, that just leaves a grey area that can be interpreted in any way, shape and form by someone else, depending on how they want to see and interpret it. Hence why, in my opinion, verbal boundaries are always best.

In many cases, we overcompensate by

becoming aggressive when people overstep our boundaries. That aggression is an accumulation of many overstepped boundaries – you've just reached your limit. If you delve even deeper, you will find that part of you that feels hurt, disrespected and powerless. As I am sure you have noticed, it's so much easier to say no when you are really pissed off than when you are in a good and happy state. Aggression is not confidence; it's an overcorrection of overstepped boundaries. Sometimes we just completely surrender and don't even try to establish boundaries. The will to establish boundaries has been completely wiped out. What is the result of this? You either overcompensate, or you don't have boundaries at all.

Chapter 2

"Those who deny freedom to others deserve it not for themselves; and under the rule of a just God, cannot long retain it." -Abraham Lincoln

Associations with boundaries

What happened the first time you said no? I am sure many of you will not have a positive response. This moment is crucial; this is a memory, whether conscious or unconscious, that can greatly affect your ability to feel safe expressing a verbal or physical boundary.

Even as you matured, you might have had negative experiences in expressing your boundaries, or in many other cases you were not even allowed to think that you had the option of expressing a boundary. There is that old saying that children should been seen and not heard.

When you expressed your boundaries, you might have been punished verbally or physically. Or you may have been made to feel shameful for expressing a need or boundary that you had. Shame and guilt always seem to be the main drivers behind people not expressing their boundaries. You were made to feel responsible for expressing a boundary that would take your mother's joy or happiness away. Meaning, if you didn't listen to your mother or caretaker, they would show disappointment in your behavior. If you didn't do what they said, you felt responsible for their emotional state.

I do discuss boundaries with children later in this book, as they can be a hairy topic. The information I am sharing is a collective experience of many clients, and there is great value in understanding these circumstances and dynamics. Because, after all, I am not here to blame and neither are you – we are here for healing and to build a healthy relationship with ourselves and to improve our quality of life. By holding onto blame, we keep breathing life back into an old deadbeat past.

This is a great exercise to establish what your

associations are with expressing your boundaries. The more aware you become, the more control you regain over your emotions and life.

Boundary Association Exercise

Ask yourself the question: "When I say or said no, how do or did I feel?" OR "How was I made to feel?" Take a few minutes or as long as you need to complete this exercise.

Saying no = _____

_____

This exercise alone will give you a very clear indication of the emotional blocks and fears holding you back from fully stepping into your boundaries, boundaries that are your birthright to have – you are worthy of them just as much as anyone else on this planet. Once you have finished making your list, carefully explore it. Read it as least 3 times. With each emotional association that you made with saying no, be present with it – where does it stem from? Who made you feel that way when you were trying to assert your boundary? It's not just important to heal the overstepped boundary itself; it is also important to heal and resolve the conflict of the relationship with the person who contributed to the stress you experienced when you tried to establish your boundaries.

These associations are stopping you dead in your tracks from expressing healthy boundaries. When you are in a situation and you need to express a boundary, these old wounds and emotions are unconsciously triggered and hinder your ability to freely express your limits. This exercise, including many others that you will be guided through, are also in my Online Healing Course for Healing Your Boundaries, Finding Peace Again, where you will not only just create these important lists (and more different exercises that will be coming up) – you will also be going through powerful healing meditations designed for the each of the chapters to help you to resolve these blocks and challenges in your life.

Using anger to set boundaries

Coming back to what I said earlier, in many cases we overcompensate by becoming aggressive when people overstep our boundaries. That aggression is a build-up of many overstepped boundaries, and you just reached your limit, resulting in a state of anger. As you have noticed, it's so much easier to say no when you are really pissed off, rather than being in a good and happy state.

Aggression is not confidence; it's an overcorrection of overstepped boundaries. Sometimes we just completely surrender and don't even try to establish a boundary. The will to establish boundaries has been completely wiped out, and that is where the danger lies. A person exhausted and depleted from being on the receiving end of the abuse, anger and intimidation has their limits. What can typically happen is the victim becomes the abuser. As you, the victim, observed the aggressor and their behavior, you learned to see the unhealthy benefit in being angry. When the aggressor was angry, you probably noticed that they were listened to, they were respected (but respected out of fear and not because they were admired and appreciated – if anything they were hated and resented). You might have also noticed that they got things done since no one challenged their boundaries or demands. This pattern will only set you up for a lonely life, potentially with people who love you out of fear and not for the sake of love itself.

You also never find the happiness and peace you are most likely searching for, since anger is the opposite vibration to happiness. Anger traps you in a state of mind that only holds grudges and resentment. It will ultimately disconnect you from your true authentic self who is meant to be peaceful and in sync with your present life, future, friends, love, family and higher purpose.

It is also important to explore what your associations are with your boundaries. Do you perhaps use anger to express your boundaries? Do you use aggression? Do you use resentment and rigidity or even resistance and stubbornness to set boundaries? All these tactics are only causing more problems, pushing people away and robbing you of your joy and quality of life. Which emotional states do you use and revert to when you express a boundary?

Expressing my boundaries = anger, resentment, rigidity, rage, yelling and so forth

I invite you to also make a list, as this will give you a deeper insight into which fears are holding you back from expressing your boundaries:

Expressing my boundaries = _____

_____

Look at the list and also become aware if you perhaps learned these patterns from a parent, authority figure or if it's from your own past, stress and trauma?

Using manipulation to set boundaries

During this section, it is important for you to recognize whether you give and support to others out of good will, or perhaps with the unconscious intention to manipulate a situation. The latter might occur because you are too fearful of asking for what you need and instead revert to manipulation in order to get what you need or want. Manipulation often excludes confrontation, rejection and abandonment – often the driving fear factors behind poor personal boundaries. Other tactics occur because ultimately we all need to express boundaries. It's the way we express those boundaries that can set the tone for how healthy they are being expressed and the desire, need and driving force behind them. This whole scenario can also be reversed.

Someone else can use manipulation to overstep your boundaries as they try to make you feel responsible for something which in fact is not your responsibility. They tend to make you also feel responsible for their happiness and can even make you feel like you are doing a good deed by giving your time and energy despite the part of you that feels resistant to their project or request. People who complain a lot, hoping that someone will come along and save them from their self-created mess, can be a trap as well. If you are too giving, be wary of this – emotionally, it is much harder to say no and establish a boundary with someone who is playing a victim role. Remember that you can only be taken for granted if you allow it. This is a pattern that can easily rub off on you, since complaining can also be a way of trying to set boundaries, but it stems from the disempowering victim state that will only cause you to alienate yourself. As you can imagine, it's not easy being around someone who complains all the time!

Also, if you are a giver and finally find yourself able to set a boundary with someone who has just taken and accepted all your time, energy and effort, they might leave your life as quickly as they came in without even a thank you – especially if they feel they were entitled to everything they received. This often stems from their childhood, where they got exactly what they wanted, or it could be the opposite – they didn't have all they needed emotionally and physically, and they are stuck in state of mind where they feel the world owes them. They will leave your life very quickly and just look for someone else who has poor personal boundaries.

Using abuse to set boundaries

People who use different forms of either emotional or physical abuse to set boundaries and get their way were often treated the same way during their childhood, and it's a deep wound that never healed. Your pain has turned into anger and a great need for you to re-establish their sense of self, your identity that was mostly likely abused and suppressed. In hindsight, you are deep down ultimately fighting to try and get your place back in life. You have learned that if you want something in life you have to fight for it, regardless if it is at the expense of someone else's quality of life and even dignity.

If you are on the receiving end of abuse, your fear toward this type of person reinforces the illusion that they are powerful and able to get away with whatever they choose to. This type of response from you only encourages, strengthens and enables this person and the cycle of their behavior.

It is crucial for you to observe how you are playing a part in this and also how you are (unintentionally) enabling it. Most likely, your compliance is due to your negative associations with boundaries and fear of confrontation. Anger is a strong emotion and enough to make anyone want to avoid it; it's a heavy negative feeling and vibration that completely disrupts one's inner harmony. In no way shape of form am I saying that you have to take responsibility for someone's behavior just because it was taken out on you and you were part of the dynamic; it is important, though, to explore what aspect in you, which emotional resource you lacked at the time, allowed this scenario to play itself out. The only responsibility that you can take is to take responsibility for your future, your emotional state and your movement forward in your life from this point onward.

Using pressure to set boundaries

Often, people can revert to patterns of using pressure as a way of setting boundaries or even to overstep your boundaries. This tactic can go two ways. If you use pressure, it's more than likely that you experienced a childhood where you experienced a great deal of stress, including pressure. This pressure could relate to feeling a great need to be perfect, always succeed, get the highest mark in school and make no mistakes in your personal life. When you finally collapsed under the pressure, punishment, judgment, rejection or even emotional abandonment followed.

The consequences of being at the receiving end of this level of pressure include anxiety attacks, tendency to abuse drugs to escape the pressure and stress and ultimately taking out this same pattern of projecting pressure onto others to get what you want. Results = Pressure.

The ripple effect of this would be to use pressure in your own life that you will project not just onto yourself but onto others as well. Putting pressure on someone in order to establish a boundary and needing to dominate occurs because you might not know how to ask for support or express your own boundaries. It is almost the same as using anger. It stems from a deep place of feeling unworthy of having boundaries respected. You can revert to a pattern that you are used to that uses anger and pressure.

The pressure compensates for the lack of

worth that you feel toward another when they feel that their boundaries are being challenged or ignored or if you need someone to help you with something but don't know how to ask for it and instead use pressure and even drama to pull people into your projects or the task that needs to be executed.

Pressure can also be felt, if you are the person asked to do something that you perhaps don't want to do. It can feel that you will not be liked or approved of if you don't comply and give into the pressure of what is expected of you. It is the same as being bullied to do something when in fact you don't want to do it; however, the consequences of not obligating is not worth it, due to your own boundary failures.

You know you are being pressured when:

- There is any part of you that feels uneasy or uncomfortable about making a decision. It's well within your right to say, "I will get back to you on that." The more you try to explain and justify yourself, the more ammunition you give the aggressor to manipulate you with.

- You receive demeaning insults just because you are not answering someone fast enough or complying with their demands, because ultimately what they want you to do relates to them. They might make you feel that you are contributing to higher cause, but let's face it: in reality it's all about this person's needs and desires.

- You feel that you have to give up your goals, dreams or plans for the sake of someone else achieving theirs. It's called self-sacrificing and it always comes at a price that is filled with regret and resentment, especially if you missed out on opportunities that could have been to your advantage, as your energy and focus is with someone else's selfish needs.

- You are ever in doubt whether you are able to perform in the way that would be expected of you. Just say no. You should never have to jump through hoops or become someone you are not in order to please someone else's demands.

Pressure is extremely unpleasant, as it creates a feeling of obligation and almost like you don't have an option to say no. The aggressor will often bombard you with so many decisions to make, deadlines and also make you feel responsible for responsibilities that are theirs to own – it should not be your problem to deal with. They tend to have an over-entitlement of delegating and turning friends into servants.

Look at people that you respect and idolize. Do they have clear boundaries? Are they able to say yes when they mean yes, and no when they chose to do so? The answer will most likely be yes, and their boundaries are also respected; they don't have to fight to be heard or respected. Their values are expressed with ease without having to attack someone else's values. In my opinion, the best way to deal with this type of people is always just say, "I will get back to you on that – I need to check with my schedule [or plans that I might have with someone else]."

Once you have set those clear polite boundaries, there should be no exceptions: stick to your boundary. If you cave in, then you let the aggressor feel that there will always be a possibility of them getting their way with you if they pressure and push you hard enough. Stand your ground; it is your right. No one has the right to rob you of that freedom to a make a decision.

Using Peace To Set a Boundary - The Unhealthy Approach

A peacekeeper can keep a confronting situation balanced and help everyone involved to see things clearly, rather than reacting from a place of anger. In my opinion, this peacemaker approach is healthy. The second peacemaker role is when you always try to keep peace even when a bully or abuser becomes angry and verbally abusive. In this case, your peacekeeper's mediating role becomes redundant; your role becomes an enabling role instead. Let me explain this point.

Let's say that your mother can be extremely difficult if she does not get what she wants. Nobody ever stands up to her. She creates drama and everyone drops everything and responds to her needs. If someone dares to challenge her, they receive verbal punishment and rejection. The familiar shame and guilt trip is the result of challenging her. If you point out how inappropriate her behavior is, this is denied. The outcome is that you are given a cold-shoulder. At this point, she has manipulated others in believing that she is the victim. But because you adopted a peacemaker role, you do not say anything and forgive her behavior.

You may excuse her behavior, saying she has had a challenging past. She is in pain and she has a reason for being manipulative, mean and a bully. You and your family realize that keeping the peace keeps your mother happy.

Looking at this example, let's explore how the peacekeeper can actually become the enabler. Firstly, the abuser gets a huge benefit or secondary gain from their behavior. No one challenges them when they become abusive or express unnecessarily harsh words. Secondly, they have no reason to take responsibility for their behavior and situation. There is no encouragement for them to actually deal with unresolved issues, which are contributing to their anger and frustration. It is easier to release anger onto an innocent person than to go down memory lane to resolve old patterns and emotional blocks. Most importantly, the abuser cannot admit their problem. As long as they are being enabled or validated to abuse or argue, it is obvious that the one complaining is the one with the problem. Which in this case is you, the peacekeeper.

Suddenly, you are the one with the problem. Because the abuser knows they will be protected, their behavior becomes increasingly reckless and hurtful. Continuing this behavior leaves them feeling safe. Due to your role as peacekeeper, you give your power away, leaving the abuser even more powerful. By keeping the peace in these situations, you sacrifice your own emotional freedom and right to be respected. Your good intentions enable the abuser.

Considering this, do you realize what high price you are paying for this role? What do you have to give up and ignore in order to keep the peace within friendships and in the family? Who benefits from your role? I doubt that you are benefiting in any possible way.

It is also important to explore what your associations are with expressing your boundaries by reverting to a state of peace. For example:

Expressing my boundaries = becoming silent, hiding, running away, becoming submissive, giving in to threats and so forth.

I invite you to also make a list as this will give you a deeper insight into which fears are holding you back from expressing your boundaries:

Expressing my boundaries = _____

_____

Look at the list and also become aware if you perhaps learned these patterns from a parent, authority figures or if it's from your own pain, stress and trauma?

Standing your ground

My clients often shriek when I mention these three words. There is only one reason why people get uncomfortable when I ask, "Why don't you stand your ground?" Their answer is that it will create confrontation. Sure it will create confrontation, because the abuser knows that by being confrontational and abusive, the other person will back down and step into the peacekeeping role – then the abuser can get away with whatever they want. Again, the peacemaker adopts an enabling role. This situation can rapidly deteriorate to the point where the peacemaker becomes a victim.

When faced with the observation that aggressive behavior is not acceptable, anger is a normal response. Yet the response of "I did this or that because I was angry" is not a valid reason. Answering in this way basically means that they cannot take responsibility and are not able to control their behavior and emotions. But this is not your problem! Yet your peacekeeper's role might support the abuser's poor excuse. By being the peacekeeper, you end up taking responsibility for the situation. Unfortunately, you support and validate the abuser's unwillingness to take responsibility for their behavior.

Let me reiterate: the abuser has to own their behavior and the way they choose to respond. Unfortunately, the abuser might try to dominate and fluster you with their short temper, sledgehammer words and empty threats. If this happens, take comfort in knowing they are trying to place all the conflict and chaos responsibility onto you. It's not your problem! Have you ever suggested anger management classes to someone who uses anger to control others? I have! It's not my job to take responsibility for another's behavior. On the other hand, if you managed to jump into bed with your best friend's wife or husband – then yes, yes it is fair to say you are part of the anger projected at you!

Why do peacekeepers take on this role?

Peacekeepers actively avoid angry outbursts and the abuser or bully knows this. They know the peacekeeper will step in to save the moment. The abuser feels safe to behave wrongfully, because they know someone – you – will take responsibility for their bad behavior. You sacrifice your personal boundaries and right to be respected.

I've noticed that peacekeepers have common fears – fear of being rejected, fear of confrontation and fear of abandonment. They also feel rewarded if they sacrifice their truth when they keep the peace. For the peacekeeper, peace means safety and peace in their environment, yet it comes at a price. Unfortunately, the reward that peacekeepers expect, is no reward. The more leverage the bully is given through peacekeeping, the more abusive he or she will get. A good intention driven by unconscious fears quickly becomes a dangerous and threatening pattern.

Confrontation is unpleasant, but ask yourself, "Do I want this pattern to repeat itself for many years to come?" No one likes conflict, but if someone's behavior is unreasonably manipulative and immorally wrong then something needs to be said. Just because the abuser happens to be your father, mother, uncle, aunt or anyone in a senior role does not mean that they have permission or any right to behave in an abusive manner. When you step aside and let them get away with their behavior, you enable them every single time. You positively validate their role as the bully or abuser.

In thinking about this, are you an enabler? If you realized that your years of good intentions actually gave the bully more power, then ask yourself now: "What stops me from changing this and standing my ground?" Is there a trauma or a fear in you keeping you from expressing healthy boundaries? Find it, heal it and reclaim your personal boundaries.

This leads us to another question: is it your job to be the peacekeeper? I suggest finding another role that is emotionally, spiritually and mentally healthy, meaningful and fulfilling. Find a role that you can benefit from in a healthy way.

In many cases people mature with the mindset that if they don't do things that are expected or demanded from them, they will lose their value and importance. We all want to feel important needed, but it should never be at the expense of our dignity, self-esteem and abandoning our boundaries and values.

It's common for peacekeepers to not know when and where to draw the boundary line between keeping the peace, pleasing people and always being the one who takes responsibility for everything, especially when something goes wrong!

When you allow someone to control you with their approval, then they have far more control over you than you would like to admit. This is a recipe for a toxic and unhealthy friendship or relationship dynamic. This person will continue to use your weaknesses against you unless you establish strong boundaries. Stick to these boundaries. Stand your ground. Explore why this person has such an emotionally strong hold on you. As there is a reason why you care too much about their approval and opinion of you. It is that very reason that is holding the boundary problem in place and a deep fear that sabotages your ability to correct the boundary failure and root causes of it.

Using ultimatums to sets boundaries

Ultimatums have the same negative ripple effect and consequences as using anger and pressure to establish boundaries. They create only resentment, making you feel that you have been robbed of your free will to make your own decisions and to express your boundaries. We all have limits, and often ignore the times when we have reached that limit —especially since taking action feels far more emotionally or physically dangerous than to express a boundary and put a stop to the intimidation.

Deal breaking ultimatums for me, for example, would be:

- You find yourself in situation where you have to choose between a friend/partner and your family. In some cases, this can actually be understandable, especially if two people are being pulled apart by their family's religious values and beliefs. In other cases, a partner might have no respect for your family and that could be a warning sign that something much deeper is lurking and could ultimately surface later in the relationship – that could even be detrimental to your emotional well-being.
- You have to choose between your partner and your friends. This is a classic way of isolating you from people who can talk any kind of sense into you and point out the aggressor or abuser's manipulative behavior.
- Always threatening you to leave you or cut off your privileges.

- "If only you could do more of _____, I will love you more" (this is called manipulative and conditional love).
- All your mistakes in the past keep coming to the surface and are used against you, despite your efforts to correct your past mistakes.
- Financially abusing your good will by creating debt that you are responsible for with the intention to punish you.
- Demanding your time by giving you ultimatums, even though you are exhausted and need a time out, and are being told you don't care about them and their needs.
- They make you feel you have to earn their trust and jump through hoops because of bad and negative experiences they had in the past, which are not your fault. You should not have to carry the burden and consequences of these experiences.
- Treating you as though are guilty of something until you have proven yourself innocent. That is a direct judgment and insult on your character, especially when it is clear that you have done nothing wrong – yet they still create a scenario that could be plausible.

In this exercise, I invite you to write down 10 ultimatum deal breakers for you. When someone gives you an ultimatum, this will help you to assess whether it's worth standing your ground, walking away or trying to resolve the conflict. To help you narrow it down even more, write them in terms of what is important and what is not.

For example, it is not acceptable when you get an ultimatum regarding the amount of time you can spend with your with your family, friends, co-workers, hobbies that you love, goals, your career etc. Take your time when you create this list – and once again, you can change the limits and thresholds as many times as you want in the future. As you change, so will your boundaries.

Exercise is on the next page.

What is your limit and threshold when an ultimatum is given to you?

Rough Draft	Most important to least
	1
	2
	3
	4
	5
	6
	7
	8
	9
	10

Respect yourself. During abusive and emotionally challenging relationships, at times that is all you have; it is important to hold onto that aspect of yourself as the foundation of where you will rebuild your sense, identity (meaning the person you truly are when you are not stuck in a victim state with poor boundaries) and newfound boundaries. As you know, respect is earned, but you have to earn that respect toward yourself as well. You will see a beautiful ripple effect of your self-respect mirrored back to you by new relationships and friendship dynamics that will start to surface in your life. Respect also goes hand in hand with having consistent and clear morals, who you are, what you stand for and what you value in yourself and your life.

Chapter 3

Your vision will become clear only when you can look into your own heart. Who looks outside, dreams; who looks inside, awakes. - Carl Jung

Having boundaries with yourself

The way we feel about ourselves is often a reflection of how we allow others to treat us. It is a result of failed boundaries – not loving and respecting ourselves enough to stand our ground and express our value and self-worth. The anger projected onto you can define the relationship you have with yourself. Instead of expressing old built up anger toward an aggressor, you tend to project it onto yourself and punish yourself. Your need for respect, love and respected boundaries may have been met with aggression or even abuse. That same treatment can start to form as part of our foundation – including the foundation that our identity, self-worth, confidence and strength of our personal boundaries are built on.

There is no point in even defining what your boundaries are going to be in the next few chapters if you are not going to make a commitment to yourself to honor, respect and live and breathe these boundaries. These boundaries are not meant to confine you or to control people in your life. They are being formed and established to serve as guidelines for you as to what you value, want and don't want in your life.

There are different types of boundaries to establish, and in this exercise you are going to establish your personal boundaries. Meaning, you will know that your boundaries are being overstepped and disrespected when you X, or when someone does not respect Y in your life. Let's start!

What are your limits? What are your thresholds? How do you know that your personal boundaries are being disrespected?

Let me start with a few examples:

- My boundaries are overstepped when someone does not respect my time
- When someone screams and yells at me
- When someone gives me an ultimatum
- When I am not given free will and a choice to participate in a project that I have no obligation to
- When I am spending time by myself and someone makes me feel their needs are more important than mine

In this exercise, I invite you to list at least 10 boundary limits. Take your time – you might go through waves of frustration, because now you are finally being confronted with how poor your boundaries have been. It's time to heal and resolve this once and for all. The good news is that you can always change your values list any way you please in future. Because as you change, so will your boundaries.

In the first column, write down a rough draft of your boundary limits. Just let it flow and do not try to organize them, as that will only frustrate you at this point. Try to write down at least 10 if you can; if you can't find 10, that's okay, you just have some more homework ahead of you. Once you have 10, write them down in the second column from most important to least important. Once you have completed this exercise, you will have a wonderful feeling of ease and peace! Get excited! Grab a pencil so you can erase something if you make a mistake, or you can write it all down on a piece of paper. Exercise is on the next page.

Respect for ourselves guides our morals, respect for others guides our manners.

Laurence Sterne

How do you know that your personal boundaries are being disrespected?

Rough Draft	Most important to least
	1
	2
	3
	4
	5
	6
	7
	8
	9
	10

Now that you have completed the exercise, you must be feeling a whole better. The more clarity and awareness you gain about what makes you tick, the more confidence you will start to develop and ultimately respect and trust in yourself.

As you look at this list in second column, also become aware of the boundary or threshold that is there. How does that boundary make you feel? There is trauma and stress that contributed to that boundary being so important to you. This means that your boundary as been overstepped too many times regarding the point you listed. I would highly recommend that you take the necessary time to heal the stress behind this boundary, since this boundary and root stress can often be unconscious drivers that can either be healthy or turn into self-sabotage.

For example: My first boundary would be to have and need my own space, especially when I am doing creative work. When I looked at the emotional charge and stress behind that, I realized that as a child I always had to fight for my boundaries and personal space. Little did I realize, this deep inner fighting instinct was also robbing me of my happiness and quality of life, because I always felt that I had to fight for everything that I wanted – including my need for space. Now, when you are in that state of mind – of always having to fight for everything – you are pushing away the very experience and emotional state that you are after, which my case was peace. When I was in my own space, I felt peaceful because I didn't have to fight for my personal space. I didn't have to justify myself to anyone. I felt safe, and all I wanted and was peace and safety. But I am sure you have come to learn that it's futile to fight for peace and safety when you use the opposite negative energy, intention and emotion to achieve your desired results. This only means that you push your desired goal even further away from you.

I had to learn to be more direct with my boundaries as well. Even now that I have established them, I realized there was no more sugarcoating how I feel when my boundaries are being overstepped. I needed to be more direct with my boundaries, but in a graceful and tactful way. There is no point in using force to establish your boundaries, because you run the risk of transitioning from victim to abuser. I do admit there are circumstances that call for a more forceful boundary; however, in this case, I am referring to a more general concept of setting boundaries in our day to day lives.

Also, now that you have established your boundaries, you have to give yourself permission to establish these boundaries. Let go of any fear that you have regarding needing this permission from someone else, because that person and their values do not matter! Anyone who makes you feel unworthy of embracing your boundaries is either a manipulator or abuser – that is reality. The quicker you can accept and digest that, the quicker you will be on your way to emotional freedom. The sad part I have often found is that people give their power away to elders or people they consider as their senior. Just because someone is older than you do not mean that they have the right to abuse you. That is an old school belief from the 60s that is so outdated right now. Now one has the right to abuse your free will, boundaries and identity – period. My father relentlessly abused me. I was 15 years old when I'd had enough and told him that if he continued to abuse me in that way, I would call the police and child services since I would be much happier in an orphanage than with someone like him. The abuse stopped.

Sticking to your boundaries

Know that it's your birthright as a human being to have these boundaries, regardless of what any other authority figure in your life has said. You have now graduated from what you learned as a child and everything that has been taught to you and even projected onto you that formed part of your personal boundaries foundation and identity. Now it's your turn to step into the driver's seat and decide what your self-worth is going to be. This is not a feeling that just randomly comes to you or just surfaces; it's an aspect of yourself that you create for yourself. It starts with you. The good news is that you get to determine what it looks and feels like. Once you have that clear intention and feeling, you know exactly what you should be working toward. You can work toward it and clear away the emotional blocks that stop you from feeling this in its entirety.

There is no point in working out all your boundaries and becoming clear on what they are and then never following through on them. When you have trouble following through on them, there are likely still unresolved trauma and blocks hindering your ability to step fully into your new set of boundaries. Without healthy boundaries, you will always find yourself in circumstances where your boundaries are being tested. There is a solution for this: healing your self-esteem and the negative experiences you had with expressing boundaries in the past.

I would also highly recommend that you resolve communication blocks and stress associated with expressing yourself, your needs and boundaries. All these aspects are touched on and dealt with during the Online Healing Course for Healing Your Boundaries, Finding Peace Again.

"Knowing your own darkness is the best method for dealing with the darkness's of other people." –Carl Jung

Make self-care a priority. If you are not looking after yourself, then you are not going to be able to show up in your strongest and fullest form for others. You will have enough energy to just be you. There can be circumstances that arise that might put you in the position where you might need to defend your boundary. However, it's important that you defend with confidence, knowing 100 percent that you are worthy of having that boundary. It's your boundary, and you don't have to justify that to anyone else.

Never violate your own boundaries, because when you do, you show others that it is still okay to overstep your boundaries. You set the foundation and the intention in place for how you are treated. It is important to have gentle consequences if someone oversteps your boundaries. Remember also that these consequences are not meant to control people; they are there to make a point to people who continue to disrespect your boundaries and test your limits.

Physical boundaries are just as important – they go hand in hand with emotional boundaries. Both greatly complement one another and cannot coexist separately. Physical boundaries mean your personal space, body, sexuality and also privacy. These boundaries set a clear indication and intention for who is allowed into your space and who is not, depending on the circumstances. Emotional boundaries provide you with emotional freedom and give you complete relief from being manipulated, controlled, abused and intimidated.

"How people treat you is their karma; how you react is yours." –Wayne Dyer

Defining Your Boundaries, One Step Further

Here are more examples of boundaries I am sharing from my research and what my students valued most in their lives:

- When I make a decision at my own pace and I will not be pressured into making one immediately
- I will not allow someone to make flimsy excuses for their harmful behavior towards me
- I will only spend X amount of time on my work and relationships and the rest on myself
- When I meet new people I will maintain my friendship circle, values and identity as an individual that is good enough just as I am
- I will never sacrifice my goals and dreams for the sake of someone else achieving their selfish needs
- I will not tolerate abusive behavior (here the students had their own limits in terms of what they perceived as being abusive)
- I will not allow jealous, controlling and manipulative people into my life
- I will never stop caring for myself because of the amount of time that is demanded from me

Remember, there is a difference between being controlling and being controlled. Having these boundaries are setting a very clear guideline for you as to how far you can be pushed without sacrificing your emotional, physical and spiritual needs. Being controlling is telling someone what to do. When you are expressing a boundary it only means that you are expressing where your limits are. Setting boundaries does not = being controlling. You are merely expressing what your values are without using force, manipulation, aggression or ultimatums.

Expressing what is important to you is healthy. Exercise this power so it's in your best interest and will not cause harm. How people respond to your reasonable set of values and boundaries is up to them; you should NEVER ever feel or be made to feel responsible for their feelings or how they respond. If you find yourself in that situation, it should immediately be a warning sign that you are walking down a manipulative path with someone who might not have your best interest at heart.

Communicating Boundaries

This is often the most challenging part! If we all were great communicators, we wouldn't have so much conflict and misunderstanding in our relationships, friendships and family dynamics. The art of communication is actually quite simple. What makes it challenging is our negative association and even trauma that we associate with it. Perhaps when you tried to communicate your boundaries, needs, values or opinions in your past they were not received well, and the backlash and responses from people that you perhaps respected made you feel rejected, isolated, punished, abandoned and even emotionally or physically abused.

Speaking one's truth is such a powerful aspect to us – this is the gateway that can open up and allow ourselves to be seen and heard by others. This is how we allow others to understand our needs, who we are and makes us "tick" as an individual being. Without communication, the entire structure and order in this world would instantly collapse! That is how important communication is – not just in our personal lives and for the sake of resolving conflict, but also to communicate, co-exist and grow as a human race. When communication is blocked, not expressed clearly or not expressed at all, then we have some serious problems to deal with.

What are your values and threshold in terms of communication? What is not acceptable, especially when you communicate yourself and someone responds in a way that is not acceptable?

Some examples for me is when:

- Someone raises their voice at me when I express myself
- Someone just flat out ignores a reasonable expression that I made regarding my boundaries
- Someone threatens to kick me out of the house if I continue to express my boundaries
- Someone tries to make me feel guilty or shameful for expressing myself

And so forth – this will already give you an idea where to start. Think back also to the times when you did express yourself and how you were made to feel when you did.

Exercise on next page.

How do you know you are not being heard and respected when you communicate your boundaries?

Rough Draft	Most important to least
	1
	2
	3
	4
	5
	6
	7
	8
	9
	10

During the Online Healing Course for Healing Your Boundaries, Finding Peace Again, we again do this exercise and a healing meditation exercise that helps resolve your blocks associated with communicating your boundaries.

It is also important to explore what your associations are with expressing your boundaries. How were you made to feel when you expressed your boundaries? I will use myself as an example again. In the past, my associations were:

Expressing my boundaries = fear of confrontation, fear of being punished, fear of being abused, hurting people's feelings, shame, guilt and so forth.

I invite you to also make a list as this will give you a deeper insight into which fears are holding you back from expressing your boundaries:

Expressing my boundaries = _____

_____

If you don't believe that you are worthy of expressing your values and your boundaries, then simply having a clear understanding of what the blocks are will help you achieve the goal of reconnecting to your self-esteem and self-respect. It is important to resolve these blocks, as this will help to set you free from old pain, negative experiences and the past that no longer exists anymore. This is also addressed in the *Online Healing Course for Healing Your Boundaries, Finding Peace Again.*

You have to believe that you are worthy of everything you have written on your lists. Your life, needs and emotional well-being are just as important as anyone else's.

"The ego is only an illusion, but a very influential one. Letting the ego-illusion become your identity can prevent you from knowing your true self. Ego, the false idea of believing that you are what you have or what you do, is a backwards way of assessing and living life." -Wayne Dyer

Healing Your Boundaries Finding Peace Again

Chapter 4

When to say yes and when to say no

Saying yes all the time

The benefits of always saying yes include the avoidance of punishment, rejection, abandonment or being alone. Most of us often had negative experiences with the word no, and instead we learned to just say yes instead. The general experience of saying no as a child tends to stay with people for a long time, well into their adulthood. The inability to exercise boundaries has consequences. These consequences reflect in people's behavior toward others and in personal and professional relationships.

People sometimes assume we all have the same boundaries. If this was the case, then wars would not happen. Aggression is often used to set boundaries. This sprouts from the behavior pattern of feeling confident enough to say no only in a state of anger. We express unresolved anger, feelings of helplessness and powerless due to the challenge of saying no. We may even have seen our parents become angry before they obtained confidence to say no. We saw a behavior pattern that served and we followed suit.

When you say yes all the time to people, you are setting yourself up as the "go-to person" when someone needs something done or when someone needs you; that is also where a dynamic in a relationship can start that can always make you feel that you are only important and needed when someone needs you to do something. It is crucial to look at why you are always saying yes and not establishing a boundary, when deep down in your heart you know you want and need to say no. If you have a fear of saying no, you might agree and come to see that you are stuck in relationships and dynamics where you feel taken for granted.

Unhealthy benefits associated with always saying yes:

- Saying yes hoping to get an exchange
- Saying yes and going along with another's request of our time and energy, hoping we will receive an energy exchange in return
- Saying yes hoping that we will receive approval, love and feel that we are important to someone
- Saying yes to manipulate
- Saying yes to keep the peace
- Saying yes to avoid a fight or being used, and so forth

When you add strings or perhaps have an unconscious expectation to do good deeds, you can actually end up pushing people away and take the good will out of your actions. I have even come to learn that some people say yes all the time with the intention of manipulating the other person once a task or "act of good will" has been completed, making the other person feel obligated to them and feeling that they have to give something back. This is often a case a boundary failure and also a low self-esteem, where the person who always says yes does not know how to ask for help, instead giving their energy with the hope that their needs will also be met without them being in an awkward position of asking for help and being possibly rejected. In this case, you are not being honest with yourself, and this can build up a great deal of resentment.

What makes the concept of boundaries so much more complicated is when we see the praise and acknowledgement that people receive who are givers. Unfortunately, this creates an unrealistic expectation of what to expect when you decide to give your energy and time to others or toward a project. The people who are also helping and supporting play a big role. There are people out there who will just take and take from you, and will never give you any form of exchange in return. You also have people (who are very far and few between) in society who will give something back to you in the form of an energy exchange.

In other cases, you might say yes all the time and be of help and support to another because it makes you important, valued, seen and needed. This pattern could even stem from a childhood where you had to take on an adult role with a great deal of responsibly from an early age, and saying no was not option – there were too many responsibilities. A parent can often make a child feel responsible for their happiness by creating a manipulative dynamic where if the child says no, the parent lets the child understand that they are making them sad by not doing xyz chores or that "mommy will be so happy if you this for me." There is another section on having boundaries with a child, as this topic can get hairier! But for now, this is just an example I am mentioning for the sake of the discussion, and many trigger points that I am trying to bring to your awareness. Saying yes all the time also puts you in the peacekeeper category. Saying yes all the time is much easier than saying no, as saying yes diminishes any possibility of confrontation, rejection and rocking the boat with someone else.

The downside to saying yes all the time is that you will start to lose your energy, feel drained and even have bouts of insomnia and chronic fatigue. There is a reason why you are always saying yes, and part of that is you don't have healthy boundaries – perhaps you don't even know what your boundaries are, and that seems to be the biggest block for most people. Not everyone had a smooth sailing childhood where they had the ability to exercise their boundaries in a safe and gently controlled way. Often, the problem starts the first time you say no; in most cases, you didn't have a positive reaction from your parent when you tried to express a boundary. In this case, a negative association in a very early stage forms with saying no. This can either set a fighting instinct into motion – making the child feel like they have to fight and rebel for their boundaries to be acknowledged – or they can move into the peacekeeper role, and just stop questioning any urge or need to express a boundary.

Watching how our parents set boundaries also greatly influences how we express ourselves when a boundary needs to be established. It begs the question: Are you acting out a pattern you copied from your parents, or are you truly following your inner guide and voice to express a boundary in a way that feels authentic to you and your personality?

This is something that I can't reinforce enough – one of the many reasons why there are so many boundary failures and people being taken advantage of – poor communication.

Saying No

Let's start off by really appreciating the underlying power behind saying no. Imagine your life and the world where the word and boundary didn't exist. Can you image what your day to day life would be like – not to mention minute by minute? No one would understand where the other person's limits, values and beliefs were.

Communicating would be a nightmare, and to be honest, the only outcome that I could see would be conflict and alienation. People use rejection and isolation as a way of setting a boundary and removing themselves from emotionally and physically invasive and challenging circumstances. Instead of just using a simple word such as NO, action would be taken instead – which would have much more of a negative impact on one's quality of life and ability to build healthy relationships and dynamics with people in one or another.

Now, because people normally had negative experiences with the word no, they tend to say yes instead. The benefits of always saying yes include the avoidance of punishment, rejection, abandonment or being alone. The general experience of saying no as a child tends to stay with people for a long time and well into their adulthood. The inability to exercise boundaries has consequences. These consequences reflect in people's behavior toward others and in personal and professional relationships.

People sometimes assume we all have the same boundaries. If this was the case, then wars would not have happened. Aggression is often used to set boundaries. This sprouts from the behavior pattern of feeling confident enough to say no only in a state of anger. These people are expressing unresolved anger, feelings of helplessness and powerless due to the challenge of saying no. We may even have seen our parents become angry before they obtained confidence to say no. We saw a behavior pattern that served them and we followed suit.

Sometimes, we know we should say no, but we unconsciously fear the consequences of doing so. Many people have a fear of saying no. Manipulative people normally sense your guilt when you say no – they use your guilt to change your opinion or answer so it is favorable for them. Why do you feel guilty when saying no? What is the benefit of always saying yes or agreeing with others? How is giving into the demands and needs of others serving you?

Normally, the answer to these questions is that saying yes avoids confrontation, rejection, abandonment and judgment. By saying yes, you are rewarded by a positive reaction, attention, acknowledgement, love and acceptance. Where in your past did you have a lack of these emotional needs? What kind of emotional reward do you get from always saying yes to others? If you resolve the unmet emotional needs and negative associations you made with saying no, saying no would come so much easier! You should not need anger or frustration as a source of power before you can say no.

You should not need to fight for your boundaries in order to be respected. You are either not expressing your boundaries clearly enough (due to an unconscious fear of saying no), or you may have had bad or negative associations with saying no in the past. It is furthermore important that you take a closer look at the people you are attracting in your life and why you are attracting them. People who love and respect you will respect your boundaries. Saying no will set a strong limit on how much you are willing to do for someone, especially if this person is only a taker.

Sometimes we do not want to say no because we respect someone too much. This is acceptable, but it does beg the question – is it a worthiness issue, fear of authority or do you choose for this person to take the upper hand within certain circumstances? Saying yes should never leave you feeling resentful afterward. When you do feel resentful, your unconscious mind is telling you that something is amiss in the way you communicate your boundaries.

Always be clear when you say no. Never say no followed by a string of explanations. You are giving the other person more power and tools to manipulate you into changing your mind. Sometimes we do not always know whether to say yes or no. I always say to people, "I will get back to you about _____," when I am not sure how to respond. What is important, though, is that you never regret or feel resentful for saying yes – especially if someone is asking you for a favor that would require your personal time.

Another good example about saying no is when someone asks you out on a date but you do not want to go. Do not say no and then explain why; you are still leaving the other person in limbo mode! They only heard why you cannot go out with them. They might think that they still have a chance to ask you out again, creating awkward circumstances for both parties. Instead, you can say, "I admire your courage asking me out, but no thank you," and that is it.

It is pretty easy to pick up on how strong someone's boundaries by the they say no. Often you can even feel the lack of confidence that is coming through when someone says no. In other cases, a person can shy away and completely even avoid saying the word no by creating a completely different topic or distraction. Then you also have the person who uses aggression when they say no, and this is a clear indication that the person has a fear of their boundary being disrespected or overstepped. They overcompensate, trying to eliminate the possibility of their boundary being overstepped.

Resistance can also be used a way of establishing a boundary without actually using the word NO, and this can cause more problems. The other person might see you as trying to be difficult, or becoming part of the problem instead of the solution. This can have a ripple effect of building up frustration in that relationship dynamic; ultimately, it can turn into a fight, during which you finally come out with the truth and say no. This means that you almost need to be in a provocative situation in order to establish a boundary, as this is how you've learned to establish your boundaries from a young age. Sometimes, people need to be pushed over the edge in order for them to express how they really feel. The anger and adrenaline give them the push and confidence they need in order to say no – even if it might be impossible for them to say no in a good mood.

Keeping an eye on those who say no to you is a great amount of power within itself. We often try to put ourselves in someone else's shoes by thinking, "Gosh, how would I feel if said no to this person? I would feel rejected, abandoned…" and the list goes on. But you have to remember that this is your projection based on how you think they might feel. Remember that we all have different experiences in life, and just because you might feel a certain way when someone says no to you, that doesn't mean that the person on the receiving end of your boundary will feel the same way. We all have different trauma predispositions, and that is also why we respond differently to stressful events and events that could perhaps challenge our self-worth. Become aware of how you feel when someone says no to you. I invite you to come to the realization that someone else might have a completely different emotional response and experience when you express the same boundary to them. This occurs because of different upbringings, experiences in life and different levels of sensitivity to being told no.

I have learned in my own experience that it's important to stay consistent with your boundaries and the way you say no. A boundary does not have to be established with aggression, anger, rejection or even a raised voice. Boundaries can be communicated in a very graceful, yet firm way. Observe how people in your surroundings respond to the word no and to boundaries. The more consistent and graceful someone can be when they establish a boundary, the clearer this person is in terms of what their boundaries, limits and thresholds are. They are much more sensitive and good at recognizing when a boundary is being overstepped, quickly rebalancing to bring harmony back into a relationship dynamic.

It is also always important to understand that

when someone says no to you, they have their own reasons and those reasons do not always have to be justified. If a person feels that they have to justify their boundary, they might feel that they are making excuses for a valid boundary that they are establishing – perhaps that you are challenging their boundary. There are some cases when you do not understand why a boundary has been instigated, and in that case, it is okay to ask why the boundary has been expressed – with the intention to help you become more aware of people's boundaries. This inquiry should never be used with the intention to try and change – or manipulate – someone's boundary.

Saying No All The Time

There is great power in saying no; however, this can become a pattern where you always say no. You don't even give someone a chance to explain what they need, or what type of support is required – your automatic answer is always no. This tends to be the case when you have completely overcompensated your boundaries. As with saying yes, it could mean that you will lose control, be controlled, be manipulated, walk into a trap that will cause you to take on more burdens and responsibilities than what you can manage. In short, often saying yes = losing my power.

Saying no all the time is easier than saying yes, because it sets you free from any possibility of being taken advantage of. This in itself is actually poor boundaries; your no response is driven by fear and feeling that you don't deserve to be respected and heard. Your boundaries may have been so overstepped, smothered, controlled or abused that saying no is the only way you can feel empowered and safe. If this is the case for you, it's important to explore the emotional driver and root trauma causing you to feel the need to always say no. As this boundary is not stemming from a place of worthiness, it's driven by old pain and past experiences.

Saying no all the time perhaps served you at some point in your life; however, you have now graduated from those old experiences and are possibly holding onto old survival tactics that do not serve your current life, circumstances and experiences. If anything, this is sabotaging you from making positive changes in your life and inviting new and healthy relationship dynamics. I acknowledge that this pattern also stems from a place of deep mistrust. It's important to explore where you lost this trust. Perhaps even re-evaluate what your definition of trust is. Most people tend to think that trust means you are being vulnerable and can potentially be taken advantage of. My definition of trust is this: Trust is a process of setting good boundaries, opening some doors and closing others and knowing that you are making the right decisions. Trust truly sets in when the body has learned to trust the soul.

It is crucial to have healthy associations with saying no. As you can see from the examples above, if saying no is used all the time to establish boundaries, this can become a negative pattern that can do more harm than good.

If you resonate with this part, I invite you to explore the unhealthy emotional drivers behind your saying no all the time. Here is an example:

Saying no = fear of losing my power, fear of being punished, fear of being abused, fear of being taken advantage of and so forth.

I invite you to also make a list, as this will give you a deeper insight into which fears are holding you back:

Saying no = _____

_____

Once you have written down the list, read and take in every emotion you wrote down. Where does that emotion stem from? What happened that made you feel that way? Is there really a possibility of this scenario playing itself out again? Are old outdated coping skills now perhaps hindering your progress and slowing down your ability to find happiness again?

Testing the waters with boundaries:

Often, when a boundary is not respected – despite reasonable and polite efforts – a more direct approach is needed. When your boundary is not respected, there might be a deeper cause and motivation behind the person's behavior who is not respecting your boundary.

It does beg the questions:

- Why is it so important for this person to overstep your boundary?
- What will or can they gain from this?
- Why does it have to be you, why not someone else?

Often, this person could also be used to just always

having you around and know that you are always available; this tends to be the case when you used to be that old person, and now you suddenly have boundaries. They might be having a hard time accepting and adjusting to the new, stronger you. In any case, the motive behind this person's behavior needs to be addressed and directly discussed in a non-confrontational way.

The worst way to approach this is to say, "You did this and you did that." That will make the person feel that you are directly attacking their character, and this will only set off a loop that will be full of confrontation, fights and arguments. Instead, say something like, "When you ask ___ of me and I said no, it makes me feel ___. Why are you so attached to me doing this for you?"

The tricky part is that if you are dealing with a manipulator or aggressor, they might try to make you feel that you are special, that they can only trust you or that you are only one who can do something. **This is where flattery should just fly right over your head**. Especially if they have never complimented you for doing something in past, yet now that they need you, they shower you with compliments. It's called flattery through manipulation.

It is your right to express to this person that you are now valuing your time and energy more – especially since you most likely were burned out in the past by having poor boundaries and you are now starting to look after your needs as well. See what kind of response you get. If this person can respect your boundary after a very reasonable explanation and even apologizes (don't push for an apology, though – all you want is to set a boundary and be left in peace). If this person threatens to leave your life, then it's time to let them go. This person will only hold you back in the future and you are already seeing serious warning signs of this already. Be smart, aware and observant.

Ultimately, you deserve to be with people who can accept, appreciate and support your personal growth. That is what life is about: change, growth and finding what makes us truly happy. You should never have to sacrifice your happiness for the sake of another's. It shows a huge incompatibility and often one that will be hard to balance out, especially if the other is rigid, stubborn and unwilling to grow as well. Also be mindful of not stepping into the "fix mode"; they are not your project, and it's not your job, responsibility or obligation to force them to grow.

Growth takes place when you are ready, and not everyone will perhaps be as ready as you are. Sometimes we have love people while they make their mistakes; however, their journey should not cost you your happiness and freedom.

> *"Your personal boundaries protect the inner core of your identity and your right to choices."*
> *–Gerard Manley Hopkins*

Giving and receiving

Giving your time or energy to someone can be a great feeling, as it is healthy to give something back in one way or another, since often people do help us and they expect nothing in return. I call this paying forward. However, even this concept does have boundaries and limits.

A good way to judge how well balanced your life is in terms of giving and receiving is to look at your energy levels. Are you tired of always giving because nothing is being given back to you in return? Do you feel burdened and obligated when someone else does something for you, and therefore you only prefer to give because it releases you from feeling beholden to someone? How resentful do you feel toward people or circumstances? The more anger and resentment there is, the more likely your boundaries have been overstepped on a regular basis without you expressing where your limit and threshold is. This is normally the case when you don't even recognize where your boundary limit and threshold is; if you did, then you would have taken action at the appropriate time.

As I mentioned earlier, the biggest mistake a person can make is to give while expecting something in return. Parents can also be a good example in this case. They invest all their time and money in a child's upbringing, school and college, and then remind them of all the good deeds and sacrifices they made in order for that child to have a good life. That dynamic alone can be good enough for this child to mature into an adult weary of receiving support, unconsciously fearing what will happen in the future if they allow themselves to receive.

The concept and definition of giving has become such a negative experience, whereas in the past it truly was a wonderful act of good will. But now people tend to give with the intention to receive, and it takes the sincerity and ability to feel safe receiving out of the relationship dynamic. This happens when a person wants to be known and seen as a kind-hearted person, yet they deeply want the energy or time back that they invested as they walked into the "giving dynamic" with someone else – with strings attached.

This leaves you in a defensive state, as good will has turned into a sour, resentful, unbalanced exchange. This does have a ripple effect on your self-esteem and how you present yourself in relationships and society, while having your personal needs met at the same time.

Giving doesn't also always have to require your physical presence or time. You can show support and your presence in different ways, such as having flowers delivered to someone, or getting them that ticket to a game or concert that they always wanted or even just a phone call to say hi and see how someone is doing.

Saying no will always create clarity where there

was once confusion; however, as in the earlier examples that I mentioned, when someone always says yes or always says no, it's important to know when to establish a boundary. You have already started to work on your lists that will help you become aware of when a request is unreasonable or just downright out of line. This will also help you to set apart the friends and people in your life who are healthy and unhealthy. You can never rule out an initial negative reaction from a friend or partner when you finally say no to them. It's how you respond after their initial response that can set off a fire or create an opportunity to find common ground. By using gracefulness and even expressing the intention that you don't want to fight or create a confrontation, you will convey that you are merely at a place in your life where you need to exercise more boundaries – that you feel tired and need more care. That includes your emotional well-being.

Exercise To Establish If What You Do For Others Gives You Joy or Brings On Resentment

A good way to establish what you can offer and give in your life without expecting anything in return or feeling resentful for spending your time and energy on someone. The best way to become aware of what you give to others and whether that makes you feel resentful or if it brings you joy will be strong indicators as boundary limits that are being triggered. Start to focus more and more on this fine line.

Start to do less things that make you feel resentful, or have a gentle conversation with the person who makes you feel resentful when you give your time and energy to them. Remember when you address this with someone else, never start the conversation with "You did this and that and this why I feel this way." Always start by saying that "I would like to discuss something with you that has been on my mind with the intention to resolve something that I feel challenged by. I only wish to have great harmony again in our relationship." Then explain that "When you do [X] or you ask me to do [Y], then I feel resentment and I feel [drained, tired, giving too much], and I need to find more balance in my life, especially what I give and receive from others."

Approach it with the intention and verbal explanation that in no way are you blaming them. You are looking for a solution with the intention to bring back balance into the relationship.

Summarized: The best way to express yourself to someone is by starting the sentence like this: "I feel _____ when you ask me to do _____." By always starting your sentences with "I feel," no one will be able to deny your feelings, even if they deny their own actions. Gently express how the person's actions made you feel. You could perhaps be facing your own challenges and this person is either not aware of it or does not take it into consideration. Never blame them explicitly, because if you do, it will provoke confrontation. Through blaming, you will create a situation where the other person will feel attacked, and a defensive reaction is sure to follow.

Also start to focus more on what you do for others that actually makes you happy and joyful without feeling that you are losing your energy or time. Acts of good will should leave that warm feeling in your heart and you'll know 100% that you don't want anything in return. And even when you do this act of good will, always have good boundaries with yourself and know and recognize what your limits are. When you feel you have hit your limit of giving, stop, take a break and shift your focus elsewhere until you feel ready to give or share your energy again.

Make a list of what makes you feel resentful and what makes you feel joyful when you share your time and energy with someone or a project.

Example: What makes me happy (this could also tie in with your language and actions of love, meaning the way you show love and appreciation to someone):

- I feel joyful when I help my partner/friend with his/her creative projects, because I learn from it and also feel creative
- I enjoy cooking dinner every night, because seeing my friend/partner enjoy the food I made makes me happy
- I enjoy surprising my partner in bed with a warm cup of coffee

What makes me feel resentful:

- When I am in the middle of an important project and I have to drop everything to help someone
- When I am in great need of rest and my need for space and rest is not respected, and demands are being made on my time

- When I want to do something for myself and feel conflicted by something I was asked to do for someone else

Exercise is on the next page:

"When you do things from your soul, you feel a river moving in you, a joy."
— Jalaluddin Rumi

What brings you joy	What makes you feel resentful?

Keep track of what makes you happy when you say yes to someone or to a project and when you feel resentful or uneasy about a request. If your list has many red entries (meaning negative experiences), then you are giving too much and not getting back what you need to keep the energy balance in a healthy shape.

"Your task is not to seek for love, but merely to seek and find all the barriers within yourself that you have built against it." - Rumi

Chapter 5

"We can say what we need to say. We can gently, but assertively, speak our mind. We do not need to be judgmental, tactless, blaming or cruel when we speak our truths" –Melody Beattie

Setting Boundaries and Healing Boundaries – Final Recap

In order to set an effective boundary, you need to be able to say no with conviction. It's no good saying no if you don't mean it or if you come across so weak that it lacks credibility. That is not a boundary.

We often feel ashamed and guilty when we say no. The guilt is formed because, as a child, you were likely made to feel bad when you said no. Saying no also brings up a fear that family and friends will reject you. No one likes being rejected, and, as a result, we suppress our boundaries with the intention of being accepted by peers or authority figures.

The way you project your boundaries immediately defines a big part of who you are to the receiver. It sets the standard of how you would like to be treated by someone. If you don't set boundaries, you leave it to the other person to decide what your boundaries are.

If you say no in a calm and confident manner, your boundaries will most likely be respected. If you say no with fear and aggression, the abuser will probably not take you as seriously, sensing you are coming from a place of fear.

Are you using old pain and trauma to establish your boundaries?

People sometimes unconsciously hold onto their trauma to keep them safe. The trauma becomes a substitute for boundaries. There are a few ways that you might confuse trauma and boundaries. Broadly, you can be passive or aggressive. The passive approach is to retreat inwards (to hide) and not take any risks. People who stay inside their house because the outside is dangerous are creating a type of boundary – but really, they are just using their trauma (related to abuse that affected their ability to express and have boundaries) in order to try to feel safe.

The aggressive approach is to use the emotional suppressed charge or tension of the trauma (such as anger, horror, fear and terror) and convert this tension to create boundaries and keep people away. For example, it is not uncommon for women who have been abused by a man to become quite aggressive and confrontational with men in general.

A common symptom of confusing trauma and boundaries is excessive weight gain. Because of a lack or failure of real boundaries, the person uses their trauma to create a shield. The body responds by adding weight as a "spare tire" to shield the person from unwanted sexual attraction, touch or intimate relationships. Setting boundaries this way is extremely unhealthy.

Instead of working on letting go of trauma, people utilize their trauma in order to keep them safe. This pattern always has a negative outcome.

Examples of boundary issues to explore:

- Someone asks you for a favor and you feel too guilty to say no, so instead you say yes, even though you don't want to do it;

- Not giving people your honest opinion; you would much rather tell them what they want to hear;

- Allowing people to make decisions for you without consulting you first;

- Having an arrogant person in your life walk all over you when they feel like it – having your boundaries laughed at;

- Feeling like you have to carry other people's problems for them;

- Finding yourself feeling trapped between your dreams and what someone else wants – and you end up giving up your dreams so your partner can pursue theirs;

- Not wanting to ask for support, with a hidden fear that it might create an obligation or commit you to something unfair or inappropriate (and then you are sitting with yet another boundary issue);

- Having trouble receiving assistance from others;
- Not feeling worthy of receiving assistance from others;
- Feeling like people are trying to manipulate your thoughts and reactions;
- Being told what to do and not asked if you would do it;
- Ongoing anger at yourself or someone else;
- Feeling the need to apologize for everything you do wrong or feeling that what you've done is not good enough (is an end result of a low self-esteem);
- Feeling unworthy of having your boundaries respected;
- Aimlessly following someone else's demands, agenda, needs, goals, dreams and even values that are in conflict with yours; putting that person in a place of power and stepping into a place of disempowerment yourself;
- Always being too busy with someone's goals and project that you neglect your own projects as the person might say we will make your

dreams come if you only help me with this, however this person never follows through on their promise;

- When you make a commitment to someone knowing full well that you are not available and then you find yourself in a situation where you have rearrange and change your milestones;

- Being and feeling dictated by people who are trying to mold you into becoming someone that they want you to be as it will serve their purpose and not yours; or

- Not communicating your emotional problems and needs to friends who can help you.

These patterns will only reinforce the illusion that you are not worthy of having boundaries.

During the *Online Healing Course for Healing Your Boundaries, Finding Peace Again*, we address these blocks and aspects that you are holding you back.

Boundaries should be a natural state. You should not have to fight for your boundaries in order to be respected. If you are fighting for your boundaries, then situations will manifest in your life that will make you feel that you need to fight even harder for your boundaries, freedom and happiness.

Remind yourself of the points below when you are faced with a situation where you need to set boundaries:

- I am worthy of having my own boundaries;
- I am a powerful being with my own unique boundaries;
- I am my own creator and creator of my boundaries;
- I choose to have my own opinions and boundaries;
- I am worthy of respect;
- I respect and love myself enough to say no;
- I value my time enough to say no; and
- I am capable of making my own decisions.

My own experiences with learning boundaries

Most of my life, I have either lacked boundaries altogether or over-corrected boundaries by using my trauma (and fight instinct) as a boundary, depending on the circumstances. I did this my entire life until I was able to process the abuse trauma.

My poor boundaries made me feel like I was

carrying the side effects of my past with me everywhere I went. I always felt violated, dirty, disgusted, humiliated, self-loathing and defensive. I indirectly expressed those emotions in my everyday life. It was an illusion that I created for myself that made me feel weak.

I wrapped my whole life around my trauma, and it created this illusion that I had no rights. As an adult, entering a very male-dominated workplace, I found that my trauma could keep me safe. I moved into the category of over-corrected boundaries, in which my fight instinct kept me safe. Of course, trauma is not a real boundary – but under the circumstances, it worked.

I have had co-workers become physically violent in my office on a construction site because one employee tried to control the other employee's area. I had to break up the fight with a chair, since their swinging fists were coming too close to me and I feared that I might get hurt. I had such a big fright that I grabbed both of them by their collars and threw them out of my office. They both lost their jobs due to the violent outburst.

My fight instinct also helped me to manage abusive supervisors. For instance, I had a boss who was verbally abusive. I once left a 500-page document on his desk with a note on it indicating where he needed to sign the cover page. He walked into his office, picked up the document and came into my office. He forcefully threw the document on my desk and said, "What the fuck am I supposed to do with this?" He turned around and walked back to his office. I looked at the document and realized that he hadn't signed it. I picked up the document and walked into his office. I slammed the document on his desk as hard as I could, pointed to the note and said, "Read it? You're supposed to fucking sign it!"

He looked so embarrassed and shocked by my response. He signed it, and from that day on, I had the utmost respect from him. He abused everyone in the office except me. Now it begs the question: Would I have attracted a boss that was so verbally abusive if I had never been abused and exposed to verbal abuse in my childhood? The answer can be complicated, but in this instance, I am going to make it simple. I believe that I would have been able to attract a much calmer and in control boss if I myself was able to be calm and in control. I believe that you tend to attract people into your life who reflect how you feel about yourself.

Given that abuse was so much a part of my life, I was not scared to stand up for myself in challenging situations. I was desensitized to it, and familiar with how to respond.

To demonstrate just how desensitized I was by the trauma, I once physically controlled a laborer many times my size and perhaps twice my age.

He had walked into my office, sat down and placed his dirty muddy boots on my desk. He looked at me and asked, "So when will you and I get together?" I have seen and experienced a lot in my life, but this was something else. I told him to get out of my office. He became aggressive and said that he would leave when he was ready. It almost felt like a vein popped in my head when I heard him say that. I got up from my chair, grabbed him by the ear and literally pulled him out of my office.

My behavior might seem aggressive, but that is how I survived on construction sites where men outnumbered women, 200 to 1. It was in my nature to defend myself when I felt unsafe. I relied on my fight instinct – and hence my trauma, to protect me.

Sure, the trauma protected me, but at a great risk. As I learned growing up in such a harsh and hostile country, standing up for oneself is not always the safest option.

What's the correct response? It's the one that doesn't come from fear or trauma. When you are in a place of clarity you know how to defend yourself and you know the difference between setting a boundary and over-correcting a boundary. It means that you set your boundaries from self-love and the feeling that you deserve to have boundaries.

Your boundaries are a reflection of your inner strength; conflict is a reflection of your inner weakness

I cannot emphasize enough how important it is to work on your boundaries. Learn to say no when you feel resentful toward a situation. You are polluting yourself by just giving into others' demands and needs. You will find that people will begin to respect you more when you say no.

An important point I've learned is that healthy boundaries and inner strength allow you to facilitate a confrontation with much less drama. It's a sign of your inner wisdom and growth. The more you listen to yourself and your own inner guidance, the stronger you become.

Chapter 6

*"The minute I heard my first love story,
I started looking for you, not knowing how blind that was.
Lovers don't finally meet somewhere.
They're in each other all along."*
— Jalaluddin Rumi, The Illuminated Rumi

Dating for all the right reasons versus dating for all the wrong reasons

People tend to think that they love someone, but deep down they are scared of being alone. Falling in love with someone sounds better in a person's conscious mind than acknowledging the reality of a deteriorating relationship or facing their worst fears: loneliness, abandonment, or rejection.

The emotional reward of plainly being with someone instead of being alone can sometimes outweigh all common logic, especially if a person is in an unhealthy relationship. They know that they are in an unhealthy relationship but they are too scared to do something about it. It feels safer being with someone rather than being alone. This is not love. It is a fear of abandonment and a fear of loneliness, disguised in the form of love. If you are affected by this situation, then you tend to misinterpret your circumstances. Although you might think you love someone, in reality, you are holding onto someone for the reason of avoiding loneliness. The comfort, emotional reward and safety received from being with someone fulfills a basic need – the need to be part of something, whether it is a relationship, community or family.

All humans have a natural instinct to feel safe, and they tend to find safety in numbers or in complete isolation. Here we are looking at finding comfort in others, such as a partner. When someone fulfills a person's need for safety and basic needs (such as a nice house, food, money and clothing), they tend to react to this partner from a deep instinctual level. The one partner covers the other's needs. But it is here that people tend to confuse the feelings of safety and caring with the feeling of being loved. Yes, a person may give and do things for others because they love them, but they are also fulfilling an instinctual need to provide. Looking for and receiving things are deeply programmed into our biology, and it ensures biological and emotional survival. Sometimes people confuse the fulfilling of these instinctual needs with being loved. We see this situation where a partner is physically and or emotionally abusive.

I acknowledge that this is not the case for everyone, but it definitely is the case for the majority of people in unhappy relationships. Now the big question: What is love? What is it supposed to feel like? How do you know that you love someone for all the right reasons? The answer?

Even I need to think about answering this, and there are a few questions that you can ask yourself to help answer this:

- Imagine taking away your fear of loneliness
- You resolve your abandonment trauma
- Now add a house, enough food, enough money, feelings of safety and security in your

environment
- Imagine these can never be taken away from you

When you look at the above list, and you had everything on that list and perhaps even more, would you still want to be with your partner? Often we fall in love with the idea that someone can provide, and that can create an attraction based on need rather than love. As if someone can provide the things that you lack in life. This type of attraction rarely turns into true deep love; it often becomes a co-dependent dynamic.

Many people – and perhaps there could be a part of you that can relate to this in one way or another, deep down – might also have a need to rescue someone. Or, perhaps you are the one who needs to be rescued, and sees a relationship as a safe sanctuary that can give you relief from your challenging experiences and circumstances. This could range from the woman who has been wounded by a so many men or the man who has been wounded by so many women. We often Romanize a relationship and think that our love can heal and repair a man or woman who can't get their life, finances or career together.

Perhaps you feel the need to be with someone so you don't have to face the emotional demons that surface when you are alone. Ultimately its not about hating yourself – it's about hating how you start to feel when you are on your own. You associate those feelings with yourself and your identity, since they can be so strong when there is no distraction from them.

You perhaps think you can help your partner back on their feet, but when poor boundaries come into play from your side, things can potentially go very wrong. People often get involved in relationships because they don't want to face their demons alone, and can pull other people into their problems and challenges. When boundaries are not being clearly expressed in these circumstances, you might find yourself with a bigger problem than what you originally had before you started dating. That is why I brought up this topic, because boundaries play an extremely important role, especially when you are trying to establish what you want in your relationships. If you are looking for a relationship hoping it will help heal you in one way or another, then in most cases that relationship will not work out. The relationship will only smooth over and cover up the deep unresolved pain that you have not dealt with as your attention and energy is distracted and focused elsewhere.

Often, your poor boundaries and fear of being alone can land you in relationship dynamic that could make you feel:

- That you are willing to put up with someone's disrespectful behavior
- Like you are changing your personality and even values with the intention to relate better to the other person
- That you're not keeping tabs on what you deserve in the relationship and settling for so much less than what you actually deserve
- Like you hang onto a relationship knowing it's not going to work, yet you still hope that it will if you give more of your energy and time
- That perhaps you are becoming too controlling toward the other person because you fear losing him or her

It's common to gravitate to unhealthy relationships, especially if that is a pattern for you or you saw that dynamic between your parents. People tend to stick to what they know, instead of venturing out into the unknown not knowing what expect. If you are used to being abused, disrespected and having your boundaries crossed, then the unconscious mind has been trained to feel more comfortable with these abusive dynamics, as you already have hard coded survival tactics (no matter how unhealthy or toxic the relationship is) that help you cope under the stress, pressure, control, intimidation and having your boundaries challenged on a regular basis.

Whereas, even if you did attract a healthy relationship, it could raise a great deal of trust issues, as there will be a part of you that feels this is too good to be true and you might find yourself almost waiting for this person to reveal the aggressor hiding under their "façade." Though, there actually are good people out there and not everyone has their goal set on overstepping your boundaries and taking advantage of you.

"Take someone who doesn't keep score, who's not looking to be richer, or afraid of losing, who has not the slightest interest even in his own personality: he's free." — Jalaluddin Rumi

True love versus friendship

Sound familiar? This has surely happened to me as well. In my experience, I found that I had what you would call a crush on someone. However, we weren't really friends – there was no really solid friendship dynamic when we started dating. I most definitely liked him in the beginning of the relationship, because he was exactly the kind of partner that I wanted. Almost like what you would see in the movies. What I didn't realize at the time was that I was attracted to what I thought he was, and also what he could become as he matured.

I realized that I projected what I saw on TV, reading romance novels onto him, and he seemed to have done the same with me. This idealization is much more common than what you would expect! This can in some cases be good, and often also bad. Meeting someone new (especially if you have met them for the first time like on a blind date), idealization tends to fill in aspects of the person you are still trying to get to know and understand. As this idealization even tends to smooth over any flaws of the other person that you might start to see and become aware of, admiration can overpower common logic – especially in the early stages of a new relationship. This is exactly what happened to me. We both ended up placing unrealistic expectations on each other, which made the relationship extremely stressful as we both tried to make the relationship work. But we only ended up resenting each other, since I didn't want to change into the person he wanted me to become, and he didn't want to change into the person I was hoping he could become.

The friendship aspect was also missing and not developing in a healthy way either. Part of his ego wouldn't allow him to open up more to me in the way that friends would do. When I say open up, I don't mean by being vulnerable; I just never saw a side to him that would make feel and say that he was also a friend and not just a lover. Shortly after I realized how lonely I felt – the friendship was missing and we were not growing together – we drifted apart. After 5 years in relationship (we both had a fear of being alone), he asked me to marry him. Before I realized what I'd said, I said yes. We were engaged for 3 months and I finally came to my senses and realized that I was not respecting my boundaries and values in terms of what I wanted in a relationship, even in a marriage. I broke off the engagement and we both felt a sense of relief knowing that this was the right decision for both of our futures.

This relationship was very significant for me. It showed me what I didn't want in a relationship; the bad times and challenges overshadowed the positive aspects of the relationship. That in itself was a clear sign that it was not heading in the right direction. I realized that you also have to have boundaries, reasonable expectations and limits in a relationship, and I found that I'd ignored every single one of them.

Not only did I need to reassess my boundaries, expectations and limits – I also explored why I had attracted this partner. His behavior was a spitting image of my father – a loud, disrespectful, cheating alcoholic who blamed everyone for his problems.

I had some homework to do. First, I looked at what associations come with a relationship.

A relationship with a man = abuse, being lied to, lack of communication, being almost a servant rather than partner, putting their needs ahead of mine, sacrificing my goals and needs in order to attend to theirs.

Now, in no way, shape or form am I blaming this partner for the way I behaved. These were my patterns, and that was why he was attracted to me in the first place. I was attracted to him too, since he fit the characteristic profile of my father and the marriage he'd had with my mother. It was almost a match made out of hell! I fully owned how I'd contributed to this; I kept enabling him and his demands, controlling nature, lies and I didn't realize at that young age that I was worthy of having a healthier relationship.

> *"Be grateful for whoever comes, because each has been sent as a guide from beyond." — Jalaluddin Rumi*

This was partly where my healing journey started. I realized deep down that I had to shift these patterns, work on my self-esteem and re-evaluate what my values and boundaries were. I had unconsciously adopted my mother's values (in terms of what a wife should be – and I have to give it to my mum, she gave it her all!), and most women in South Africa tend to suffer from low self-esteems since there is a strong mentality that the man is the leader and the wife and children are only followers

– anyone who steps out of that line of expectation will see consequences in one way or another.

I started to resolve my associations with relationships, men and being a female partner to a man. I also re-evaluated my boundaries, thresholds and expectations in a relationship.

How do I know that my boundaries are being overstepped in a relationship? I created my own threshold limit:

- When I am yelled at
- When I am told what to do without the person having any regard for my well-being and needs
- When I have to drop everything to help someone with their goals while I am busy with mine
- When I am not able to sleep in after working an 85-hour week
- When I cannot wear what I want to wear and so forth

Now, I invite you to make your list (on the next page)

How do you know you are not being respected in your relationship?

Rough Draft	Most important to least
	1
	2
	3
	4
	5
	6
	7
	8
	9
	10

As you are looking at this list in second column, also become aware of the boundary or threshold that is there. How does that boundary make you feel? If there is trauma and stress behind it, it's strong enough to be at the top of your list and I would highly recommend that you take the necessary time to heal the stress behind this boundary; this boundary, and especially the root stress behind it, can often be an unconscious driver that can either be healthy or even turn into self-sabotage.

> *"Be melting snow.*
> *Wash yourself of yourself."*
> *— Jalaluddin Rumi, The Essential Rumi*

It is also important to explore what your associations are with expressing your boundaries to a man or woman. How were you made to feel when you expressed your boundaries? I will use myself as an example again. In the past, my associations were:

Expressing my boundaries to my partner = fear of confrontation, rejection, threatened to be abandoned, attached, abused etc.

I invite you to also make a list, as this will give you a deeper insight into which fears are holding you back from expressing your boundaries:

Expressing my boundaries to my partner = _____

___

Now that you have completed the exercise, you must be feeling a whole lot better. The more clarity and awareness you have of what makes you tick and the issue blocks behind your boundaries conflicts, the more confidence you will start to develop and ultimately respect and trust in yourself.

> *"Let yourself be drawn by the stronger pull of that which you truly love."* —Jalaluddin Rumi

Now, another aspect to boundaries can be what your expectations are of a partner. Meaning, if he or she does not have these qualities, then it's a deal breaker. It's also important to have list of habits or patterns that you can tolerate in a partner.

Let's start with the deal breakers. Here are some examples:

- If the person is a drug addict
- Has aggression problems

- Show signs of potentially becoming violent
- Lies and cheats (disrespecting my values and the kind of relationship I want, in this case a monogamous relationship)
- Shows an inconsistency in their belief system and values
- Mood swings that are projected onto me and I am made to feel responsible for it
- Feeling responsible for this person's happiness, etc.
- Having to give up on my beliefs and values to fit in with this person's beliefs and values
- Being asked to give up the time I spend with my friends

Now I invite you to make your list (on next page).

"Sorrow prepares you for joy. It violently sweeps everything out of your house, so that new joy can find space to enter. It shakes the yellow leaves from the bough of your heart, so that fresh, green leaves can grow in their place. It pulls up the rotten roots, so that new roots hidden beneath have room to grow. Whatever sorrow shakes from your heart, far better things will take their place."
— *Jalaluddin Rumi*

What are deal breakers in a relationship?

Rough Draft	Most important to least
	1
	2
	3
	4
	5
	6
	7
	8
	9
	10

Make a list of things that can you live with. Here are some examples:

- They can sometimes be disorganized

- They can be forgetful of important dates such as my birthday (this has happened to almost everyone)
- Trying to appear stronger than what they actually are to impress me
- Avoidance of closeness, this often starts to fade the better they get to know me
- Being overly tidy and always trying to do things the right way

I invite you now to make your list. In this exercise, it's not necessary to rate them from most important to least important:

_____

_____

_____

_____

_____

_____

_____

_____

The last exercise for this chapter is making a list of qualities that you would like your partner to have. Also be realistic with what your expectations are; remember that you also have your flaws and the other will also have their quirks – hence why you created the list of what you can accept.

Here are some examples:

- Funny
- Able to keep the communication channels open with me when we go through challenging times
- Able to supportive toward me just as much I am supportive to them
- Honesty
- Fidelity
- Teamwork and so forth

Exercise on next page.

"If you find me not within you, you will never find me. For I have been with you, from the beginning of me."
— Jalaluddin Rumi

Qualities you would like your partner to have. This is still part of your boundaries, with a different angle:

Rough Draft	Most important to least
	1
	2
	3
	4
	5
	6
	7
	8
	9
	10

Important points to remember: Don't be their parent, be a partner! When you look at the bigger picture of dating, it does boil down to that need for love and to be loved and to have companionship in your life. However, the emotional drivers driving this desire and need can make it either healthy or unhealthy. The clearer you are about the exercises above, the clearer you will be as to why you are searching for that special person.

When you resolve the blocks you have come up with, you stand a much better chance of finally recognizing the ideal partner for you. When there is a blurred line in your boundaries and how to express them, you give too much of yourself and before you know it, your relationship drains you completely. You find that you have stayed in this hopeful state of mind only to realize that the other person has just been taking, accepting and even abusing your good will.

Your love and ability to love is part of who you are. When you share this aspect of yourself, you want to share it with someone who will be able to receive it and also complete the energy exchange cycle back to you in their way (meaning, their language of love). When there is an equal give and take, the energy in the relationship always flows. It creates a safe place and space for two people to communicate and come together, work together and also work separately, maintaining each other's individuality and freedom.

It's not your job or responsibility to coach or heal someone. Everyone is responsible for their own healing journey, and they have free will to choose to change or not. No one consciously is going to look for someone who is going to be a challenge with and make them unhappy. No one really goes out into the world and look for someone to abuse their boundaries. However, when we often meet someone love can affect our commonsense and make us feel that if there is something in this person that is greatly challenging you in a negative that perhaps you can help, save or change them. This type of relationship dynamic will fail 100 percent guaranteed as you can make the other person feel that there is always something wrong with them and they are not good enough; this will only lead to resentment, anger and hurt feelings, which can turn into abusive words and even actions. Or, this person can become so dependent on you that you end up with a needy partner instead of a partner who is an equal to you.

"Yesterday I was clever, so I wanted to change the world. Today I am wise, so I am changing myself." — Jalaluddin Rumi

Be Honest

Be honest with your partner about what you want and don't want in a relationship. This exercise is really easy if you can get your partner to make their own lists like yours, so you can exchange them and discuss any big differences. Here is the golden rule: be honest! Don't sway from your values and boundaries just because they could be in conflict with your partner's –that is why you did this exercise with them in the first place, to iron out differences before they become a problem. These differences can normally be dealt in a graceful way without confrontation.

"Raise your words, not voice. It is rain that grows flowers, not thunder."— Jalaluddin Rumi

However, if you do find yourself in a situation where you have a deal breaker at the bottom of his or her list (for example: you value fidelity the most and he or she is open to open relationships), you are not in the right relationship! You will have to sacrifice such a big aspect of yourself and what you stand for that you will end up resenting your partner one day. The sacrifice will come back and bite you. It will cause a tremendous amount of damage to your self-esteem and identity, and you might find yourself back at square one. That is why I can't emphasize this enough: stick to your boundaries and be loyal to them! They are there to help you achieve the ideal relationship that will complement you and your future.

Always be clear what your intention is with the relationship at the right time. Are you looking for possible commitment, or you are just going through a dating phase? Be clear with your boundaries and communication so you do not hurt yourself or the other person. Also be clear about intimacy, especially in a new relationship. In today's modern society, it's often common for people to be intimate on the first date, but this is not the case for everyone. You have every right to establish an intimacy boundary; you don't have to follow the crowd, respect yourself and also your body.

When opposites attract

This happens when you meet someone and they have such a strong quality that you lack within yourself that you fall head over heels, completely ignoring perhaps the other 95 percent of incompatibilities you have.

Here are some examples:

- He has a lot of money, I love to spend money
- He is so strong and I am so weak and vulnerable
- He is such a good provider; I can barely keep up with the bills
- He is such a good communicator and he says everything I can't say
- He or she completes me

When you get involved in this type of relationship, you run a very big risk of becoming codependent on the other person. They will only reinforce the weaknesses that you feel, causing you to feel that you cannot live without them. However, when the going gets tough and you finally realize that this relationship is based on unmet needs that you have, you might find yourself in a loveless dilemma! Never ignore these signs, as they can send of you off on a very short-lived fairy tale that will most likely not have a good ending.

"Be empty of worrying. Think of who created thought! Why do you stay in prison when the door is so wide open?" — Jalaluddin Rumi, The Essential Rumi

Chapter 7

"Words are a pretext. It is the inner bond that draws one person to another, not words."
— Jalaluddin Rumi

Boundaries in marriage

Marriage can be a beautiful partnering between two people who come together to share common goals, dreams and to also exist as two separate individuals. We all have different definitions of marriage, and my definition is what I just described. Because of our different views on marriage and what marriage should be like, you see households and partnerships that look different than other married couples. The reason for this? They have different definitions of what marriage is. When two people share the same definition, you see a happy couple. When you see two people who have very different definitions of what a marriage is, you see a lot of problems in that marriage. Because instead of two people co-existing in harmony, you see two people fighting for their values, beliefs, goals and dreams. What was meant to the start off as teamwork has become a separate journey on both sides. It is crucial that this definition is established before committing to someone.

If you haven't read the chapter that I wrote in this book about boundaries and dating, I would highly recommend it – I share vital points there as well. It is important that you choose a partner for all the right reasons. Often, we mistake being taken care of financially for love. Or, we might feel that we are loved by someone because they take care of all the responsibilities in the house.

Marriage can work between two people, only if they both share this same understanding and feeling. Being taken care financially might make you feel loved; however, what about the emotional aspect that also comes with being a marriage? What about open communication? What about honesty and openness? You see the list can go on and on.

What you build in the beginning of a marriage is often what sets the tone for the lifespan of the marriage, unless you have the cooperation of the other person to make changes with you when your initial intention for the marriage and partnership does not work out. This tends to be the case for many people!

Often, one person does not want to work on the marriage anymore; they don't want to spend more time and energy trying to find a common ground in the marriage and they inevitably give up. But normally, people give because they are searching for a few aspects that are missing in their marriage. This can be resolved with open communication and a willingness to compromise, provided that the requests are reasonable and within your values. Meaning, a request from a partner should never make you feel robbed of your identity, dignity and self-respect. That is not a partnership; that is selfishness and a boundary failure on your part. We will get to the boundaries aspect shortly.

Leaving the 95 percent for the 5 percent

A partner might leave a marriage because they are in search of that 5 percent missing in the marriage, and they leave the 95 percent behind. They come to find that when they finally do find the 5 percent, they have made a big mistake – the 95 percent of what they had is gone. In hindsight, it was better working on the missing 5 percent than walking away from the 95 percent, which is not the easiest to find in today's society.

Now, how do you avoid this? It's called boundaries. Having boundaries in a relationship, boundaries with your values, boundaries with your expectations and boundaries with your partner's expectations. The clearer these boundaries are communicated to one another, the stronger the foundation you'll have for your marriage to thrive and grow on. There will be a mutual understanding, mutual respect for each other once you both can agree and perhaps reasonable compromises for one another's boundaries, values and needs. Because ultimately, the reason why marriages fail is the lack of clarity in one's boundaries, values, emotional thresholds and limits. You might see a lot of symptoms as to why the marriage failed, but when you dig deeper and look at the root cause as to why it failed, you see that it boils down one's boundaries, values, emotional thresholds and limits that have been overstepped. Communication is powerful.

You might know your partner extremely well, but that does not mean you know how to fully communicate with them so they hear and understand what you are trying to say.

Communicating Your Boundaries

The first and foremost point here is to never ever blame – even if the partner did do something. The moment you blame your partner, they step into defense mode and will not fully hear what your message is.

If your partner is stubborn and resistant when you try to talk to them, no matter how hard you try, follow this dialogue: "When you are so resistant and stubborn, it makes me feel shut out, ignored and like this marriage is not worth improving. I want to improve things, but I can't do this without you, and your stubbornness is making this much harder on me to reach out to you and find a solution."

Conflicts and problems will usually have bubbled up after the "honeymoon" phase. This is because couples realize that the united force might not be as strong as before. Hence, they might be thinking about leaving their current partner to find that intense feeling of love. What they do not know is that achieving oneness is easy initially. The real problem arises during maintaining the oneness for a long period.

Completing versus Complementing Each Other

Marriage is not meant to complete an individual. On the contrary, it is for two complete individuals to form a commitment to each other. It is something sacred. When you feel that someone completes you, you have not fully discovered your true authentic self. You are a complete, whole being. You were born whole. Life experiences can suppress those beautiful aspects that you had fully intact the day you were born. However, the good news is that those aspects are only suppressed – they can be recovered again. It's just a matter of making a choice. Do you want to? People are often scared of their greatness, and they can even hide behind their partner, using them as an unconscious excuse to not step into their full self. Nothing bad can ever happen when you step into your power and true authentic self; it's a matter of feeling worthy of reclaiming that for yourself. A partnership can be healing; however, that is only the starting point. The rest of the healing journey will be up to you, as no one is responsible for your healing or my healing journey. It's our free will to choose that path or stay as we are.

Here are some traits of a complete individual:

- Feeling comfortable showing vulnerability through emotions
- Being assertive and in control
- Having goals and the passion to succeed
- Having a sexual interest, eagerness to learn and improve as well as being responsible

Sound like a challenge to find this person? Not if you are compatible and able to work together toward goals while maintaining your individuality. As I have mentioned before, these are just ideal traits; if a person does not have some of them, they can develop them. However, never get involved with someone because you are in love with their potential. We all have free will, and that person might choose a completely different route – make sure you can live with that and still love and support that person! Marriage occurs when you agree to merge with another person to enhance both of yourselves, together – not because of what you are hoping it can become. The marriage should already be rich enough of love, emotions and communication; you should be ready to accept it and step into it. It is the journey, not the destination, that will bring you happiness.

Remember that if you are empathetic, you are also sensitive to other people emotions and needs. You might even find that you give too much in a marriage and you are more about your partner's feelings than your own – including even your own well-being! People who are empathetic do run a higher risk of being with someone who is a manipulator, as they tend to be more concerned about how someone else feels. They have a tendency to give too much, do too much for others and get taken advantage of all the while – even though they think that they are lending a helping hand. The reason for this pattern is also because we bring so much emotion and feelings into a relationship. After all, it's our emotions that cause us to feel attracted to one another. Often, a partner does not share the same amount of intense emotions. It can be easier for someone who has less feelings for another person to become a manipulator, since they feel they need more or something different than what their partner can give. They also see an opportunity to have unreasonable needs met, whereas they would not have been met by someone with healthy boundaries.

Manipulators do not take responsibility for:

- Their feelings
- Their attitudes
- Their actions

Whereas people who have healthy boundaries – or at least a sensitivity to others' emotions – do take responsibility for their feelings, attitudes and actions.

The reason why these 3 are highlighted here is because they are the foundation for marriage. For example, let's say you and your husband often share a heart to heart talk at least once a week. I can guarantee that it will be a much healthier relationship than a marriage where there is little to no communication. Couples who share their feelings with each other tend to connect on a deeper level.

Another downfall for marriages is attitude. For instance, if a husband comes back home in "work mode," his wife might feel that he uses her as a punching bag. She prepared dinner, cleaned the house, made sure his shirts were impeccable, and yet she gets the cold shoulder. In the long run, this can turn into resentment, and they will realize only after a few years what went wrong between them. You would think that something big always has to happen in order to bring about a divorce. However, in reality, it is the accumulated little bad attitudes that cause the break up between two individuals, as there was not clear communication and boundaries.

As the old proverb states, "Actions speak louder than words." From this proverb, you can safely come into the conclusion that sometimes just saying "I love you" does not have the same impact as, say, buying flowers on a random day to show you care. A lot of people think women are after expensive items – that is false. What women really want is to feel appreciated, cared and loved by someone who shares these emotions. However, not all men want to share that level of emotional bondage. This can bring about a great deal of conflict in the relationship that can surface as smaller, unrelated problems start out as a small snowball that runs down the hill; we all know what happens to that snowball. Communication and healthy boundaries avoid this ripple effect.

What if your relationship is falling apart?

After some time, you may forget why you are

together or even got together in the first place. Resentment, disappointment, anger and rejection (just to name a few) could take the place of love, admiration, compassion and tolerance. These feelings don't just come about for no reason; there is often a build to these emotions. The reason why they are there needs to be explored. This will help you find the root cause of where you failed to communicate a boundary, value or need that you had; for example, you perhaps feel you are not respected. Hence, without clear communication – which includes values, boundaries, needs, desires and expectations – you are bound to hit a hard wall at some point that could potentially ruin the relationship.

Was it due to boundaries, values, desires, needs and so forth not being respected? Re-evaluate your values list with your partner to see where you could have missed the warning signs. Think back and, if possible, talk to your partner to reminisce about the past. This is a healthy step toward a long-lasting relationship.

Here are some areas that couples find difficult to be honest about:

- Know what kind of marriage you want; will it be

an open marriage or a monogamous relationship? In most cases, people chose a monogamous relationship since it can minimize extraneous emotions such as jealousy.

- You should make a list of your values as a monogamous partner; what does a monogamous relationship look and feel like to you? What will you tolerate in this relationship, and what will be a deal breaker?
- If you are in a monogamous relationship and you feel you are on the brink of having an affair, talk to your partner before you break your vow and the trust of your partner. Or find a trusted friend you can talk to and ask advice from; often, the problem can be so obvious, but if you are in the middle of the problem, it is not easy to see what went wrong or started to go wrong in your marriage. If your partner is part of the problem, which they (unbeknownst to them) could be, open communication with the intention to resolve this challenge is what is going to resolve this.

Common actions that can be the beginning of a potentially challenging problem

Let us observe this scenario. A man confides in his friend, explaining that he is unhappy in the relationship. His partner confides in her friends, telling them that she is unhappy about a problem in the marriage. The good news is, the problem is being communicated – but it's being communicated to the wrong audience. How will these two people resolve their conflict? Not in the near future; not unless the problem becomes so big that it has pushed the marriage into a very challenging phase.

Emotional intimacy makes marriage expose us to external forces. Once we are intimate with another person, we will see both the positive and negative traits of our loved ones. We will not really understand our spouses if we do not get to know their flaws and accept them. As a loving spouse, it is crucial to not try to change them and make them a mirror image of you. That is not the purpose of a marriage. If you have this mentality, you should change it – you're certainly not ready for a higher form of relationship.

Here are some examples of unhealthy boundaries:

- Using isolation to withdraw from a problematic situation and not communicating and resolving it; you are becoming part of the problem instead of the solution.
- Giving someone the silent treatment. Silence

should never be used as a form of punishment or a way to set a boundary; it only creates even more uncertainty, confusion and even provokes a rebellious reaction from your partner, which only creates a loop that continues an unpleasant situation.

- Using anger and raising your voice to get your point across. It's not always that the other person does not listen; it can also be the way that you communicate, which could cause them to emotionally shut down. Or, the way you communicate is perhaps clear to you, but not to the other person.
- Ignoring a problem and hoping that it will resolve itself. I can tell you now that it will not.
- Using nagging and threats. Your partner will start to secretly resent you, and if this continues on a regular basis, it could ruin the relationship.
- Using punishment as a form of boundaries, such as stopping chores you agreed to do, or going without sex and so forth. You create only more distance, and the problem becomes more than what it initially was.

Clear communication is crucial in any relationship and marriage. Without communication, you are setting yourself up for disappointment and potentially a great deal of loneliness. You will know there is a partner in your life, but that will not be enough to fulfill the emotional side we all have. You can understand someone else's opinion and point of view while you keep your opinion and point of view fully intact. Understanding someone's value or belief doesn't mean you have to agree with them; at least try to understand first.

Establishing Boundaries in a Marriage

This exercise goes two ways. If you are in a marriage, I would highly recommend that you do all these exercises with your partner, even if you have been together for years. You might be surprised to learn that you have missed a few vital points important to your partner, and they might also come to learn a few things about you that they have misunderstood all this time.

What is your definition of a marriage?

_____

_____

What do you want from a marriage? This is crucial! A wishy washy idea is not good enough – it is a recipe for a weak foundation that you build your marriage on. If you are not 100 percent sure of what you want, you will never know what you could end up with. Clarity far outweighs regret.

_____

_____

How should your partner make you feel? (be reasonable with this list; as I mentioned before, people idolize movies and romance novels – we live in reality).

_____

_____

Now, let's establish clear boundaries that you will have in the marriage. Meaning, if your partner does not comply with these policies, compromise and a serious discussion will be needed.

For example:

- If my partner cheats on me
- When my partner yells and screams at me
- When I am humiliated in public and even home
- When I am verbally insulted
- When my time is not respected

Now it's your turn to create your list. It's best to do this with your partner so you can work on this to understand on a much deeper level.

What are deal Boundary Breakers for in the Marriage?

Rough Draft	Most important to least
	1
	2
	3
	4
	5
	6
	7
	8
	9
	10

I can't emphasize enough. Clear communication is crucial in any relationship and marriage, without communication, you are setting yourself up for disappointment and potentially a great deal of loneliness. You will know there is a partner in your life, however in most cases that will not be enough to fill full the emotional side that we all have. You can understand someone else's opinion and point of view while you keep your opinion and point of view fully intact. Understanding someone's value or belief doesn't mean that you are or have to agree with them, at least try to understand first.

You can understand someone else's opinion and point of view while you keep your opinion and point of view fully intact. Therefore, understanding someone's value or belief doesn't mean that you have to agree with them; all you have to do is try to understand them at the very least and work on finding a common ground with your partner. You are married, and as you know, marriage takes work; it's not always a walk in the park. However, that does not mean you can't find the peace and harmony within that you both deserve.

"Goodbyes are only for those who love with their eyes. Because for those who love with heart and soul there is no such thing as separation."
— Jalaluddin Rumi

Healing Your Boundaries Finding Peace Again

Chapter 8

"The more severe the dysfunction you experienced growing up, the more difficult boundaries are for you."
—David W. Earle

Boundaries with kids

Having boundaries with children is probably one of the most challenging topics, since everyone has their own idea of what is good and not good for their child. These values on raising a child can stem from either trauma they experienced with their parents and it being repeated again. Or, the parents are trying to fix and overcompensate for the mistakes their parents made which can a good or bad outcome. For example, if a parent only experienced control and abuse and they trying to provide the opposite experience for their child, then they might give their child too much freedom and not enough experiences and practice with boundaries. On the flip side of the coin the parent might unconsciously be repeating patterns they experienced with their parents. How this plays out depends on the upbringing of the parent. Boundaries and love for children tend to go hand in hand.

The topic of love tends to be complex because we all have different values and beliefs. What one person think is true love is something completely different for another person. Sometimes, someone might "love" someone out of fear. This tends to be true for children who are raised in stressful circumstances. I know that I "loved" my father out of fear as child. My dad only noticed me when I did something wrong. Even though he gave me negative attention, my need to be acknowledged by him was at least met. My need for love was met by negative and even abusive reactions. This is like being programmed with incorrect reference points, due to trauma. Compare this situation to linking wires in a machine but with wrong wiring connections – the machine will not explode, yet it will not work very well either. For me, attention and love from my dad equaled abuse, anger and aggression.

If such a pattern of punishment in response to the need for love persists, children will start to associate bad behavior with attention. The child unconsciously adjusts their behavior to get more attention by misbehaving. It is at this point where the child makes the destructive association that misbehaving and provoking people results in receiving attention. Sadly, this child is not experiencing a positive reaction from one or both parents, or others. The child usually accepts this type of reaction from the parent. This destructive association tends to play itself out later in adult life, causing relationship conflicts. This negative association also affects their ability to love others for all the right reasons and not out of fear of punishment, loneliness or rejection. A child instinctively relies on his or her parent for shelter, food and safety. During the child's forming years, he or she "loves" the parents because their basic needs for survival are met.

Poor boundaries can often start in a person's childhood – not in all cases but in most cases. Parents don't give children enough emotional space and freedom to exercise saying no, though the reason why varies from family to family. Every household has its own burdens, stress and challenges to get through – a perfect parent does not exist. You can't always get it right, no matter how hard you try. We are humans and we make mistakes, period. It depends on how hard you are going to be on yourself when you make a mistake. If you were not allowed to say no during your childhood, then you might have found it challenging to set boundaries as an adult. Knowing and understanding this as an adult already gives you the upper hand in understanding the consequences that can follow when you don't have enough freedom in this area of your life.

What happened to you when you exercised saying no to your parents as a child? I remember getting a smack followed by an intimidating brawling voice from my father bellowing, "What did you just say? You have no right to say that to me!"

Unfortunately, many parents think that they own their children. In my opinion, this isn't true. In my opinion, no one owns anyone. Parents are responsible for their children; they are their guardians and teachers. It is the parent's responsibility to help their child understand what boundaries are in a healthy way. Parents should also create opportunities for the child to say no. Parents are also there to instill in the child that they are worthy of saying no. It is safe to say no. They need to understand that saying no does not always mean that they are going to be punished or attacked for expressing an emotional discomfort they are feeling in one way or another.

Children need to experience their own boundaries by learning to make decisions – provided they are not going to put their life in danger.

I know some parents are shocked by the suggestion that they should encourage and reward their child for saying no. This comes at a cost or inconvenience to the parent. The same parents who refuse to accept a child's boundaries also ask, "Why is my child [in this case an adult] in unhealthy relationships or being abused by others?" It seems that parents are shocked that after years of punishing the child for saying no to them, that the child failed to develop healthy boundaries in order to say no to others – and suddenly they are being taken advantage of by abusers, bullies and aggressors.

Boundaries start at home, with the parents. The child needs to have discernment to know when they are allowed to say no. In other words, they need boundaries to their boundaries. **Consistency** is very important.

I have had a father (a client) say to me once that he couldn't understand why his daughter was dating such a "bad boy" who did not treat her well. I thought that I would point out the obvious by asking him, "Did you ever allow your daughter to say no to you?" His answer was "No, she was just a child." I asked him why he expected her to exercise boundaries and say no to this new male figure in her life. She was never able or even allowed to say no to a masculine figure. I told him, "Your daughter was never able to exercise and establish her boundaries toward a man." He looked stumped, went pale in the face, and with an embarrassed look nodded his head, indicating that he understood the message I was trying to get across.

Children learn about boundaries from an early age, as early as the day they were born. Physical boundaries are explored during and right after birth, as they are suddenly exposed to different materials, blankets, being touched by strangers and wrapped in blankets and diapers. Then, as the baby matures, they start to learn to share their space, whether this is in a daycare center or sharing their toys. They learn where their territory is and what they perceive to belong to them. Sharing is not common sense at this point, hence why can they start to cry when an object they have been playing with is suddenly taken away.

They do not understand the sudden change and why the object they found wonder in is taken away. In time, a child will learn that it is okay to share, especially if there is an abundance of toys or objects that the baby can occupy itself with. The child is not necessarily attached the specific object, as he or she is too young to even identify what it is – it is merely the physical attachment and moment of exploration they had with that object. It's the disruption in the emotional and brain activity that they experienced with object at that time. It's the same concept when a child matures and grows attached a blanket, doll or other type of toy.

It's the physical attachment and moment of exploration they have with that object combined with the feelings of security and safety, as the brain has now developed to the point where it recognizes when it needs to feel comfort and safe. When adults are not close by to provide the level of comfort the child needs, he or she tends to latch onto what is closest to them, then forms an association with the object. For example: blanket=comfort / doll=comfort and so forth.

As the child matures, he or she will learn more about sharing. For example, if the child is at school and the child next to them asks if they can use a pencil with the agreement and understanding that the pencil will be returned. When the pencil is returned, the child starts to understand that trust can be formed and that if they share they will get their possession back. What made the child more willing to share was that he or she was consulted first.

Boundaries Exercises

If you are a parent, this exercise will be wonderful and hopefully give you a more solid guideline to help you and your child exercise boundaries in a way that does not flip your day upside down!

As the parent, decide what your thresholds are going to be with your child. Where are your limits?

Here are some examples from other parents, what is OK:

- When they want to go to bed 10 minutes later, BUT they have to get up 10 minutes earlier in the morning
- There are only designated areas on the wall they can draw on (when cardboard or special paint has been applied, where they can draw to keep them busy or as a fun reward)
- They can have desert before dinner once a week on an agreed day of the week (keep this consistent)
- One day per week, your child can decide what you do with them for at least 2 hours, provided that the request is responsible – what is reasonable needs to be explained to the child as well and so forth.

I invite you now to make a list of boundaries are OK to be flexible with, and then rate them from most important to least important. And yes, I know this is going to be frustrating, but also extremely freeing and rewarding when you feel clearer on this topic. Trust me.

Exercise on next page.

> *"Children are educated by what the grown-up is and not by his talk."* – Carl Jung

Rough Draft	Most important to least
	1
	2
	3
	4
	5
	6
	7
	8
	9
	10

Here are some examples from other parents, on what is not OK:

- When a child expresses a boundary regarding an activity or chore that they know they are not allowed to, as this has already been communicated to them
- Behaving disrespectfully at the dinner table
- Waking up more than twice per night, waking you up
- Not getting ready in the morning on time (I have heard of parents who dropped their children off at school in their pajamas because they wouldn't listen – and yes, my mum did this to me once and that is all it took; I was ready every morning after that)

Exercise on next page.

Parents are the ultimate role models for children. Every word, movement and action has an effect. No other person or outside force has a greater influence on a child than the parent. Bob Keeshan

Rough Draft	**Most important to least**
	1
	2
	3
	4
	5
	6
	7
	8
	9
	10

Bad habits as a parent to rethink:

- Inconsistency in child's routine
- Labelling their behavior good or bad (it has long-term consequences on a child's self-esteem when they are always labelled bad, and this will be come to bite you when they reach their adolescent years)

- Not having clear and consistent rules in the house
- Saying bad or negative things about the other parent. Your child is like a sponge and absorbs everything in his or environment. The more positive feedback and experiences they have, the stronger their confidence in themselves will be. One parent's mistake should never be projected onto a child – **it is not their burden to carry!**
- Don't speak to your child as if though they are stupid or slow. Speak to them in simple plain language without the baby talk tone in it; a child can feel when you are undermining them
- When you correct a child's behavior, never ever stand at our height with a finger pointing in their face. Move down to the floor so you are at their equal height; it relieves any feelings of stress, intimidation and overwhelm. You will see that they are able to digest and understand what you are trying to say much more easily
- You can't have a tantrum with your child. A child literally does not have the same emotional control as an adult does, period. Hence why it can so much harder to communicate with them and establish boundaries

- The rest is up to you as the parent to discern

Also know that you as the parent is good enough. Your efforts are good enough. You can't always be perfect! Your child is a part of you and not your entire life. If your child is your entire life, then you cease to exist. If you are not doing well emotionally, physically, mentally or spiritually, then your child will also suffer the consequences. The benefits to attending to your own needs are just as important as anyone else's. If you are happy, then everyone else in your house will also be happy!

Positive affirmations for parents:

- I am willing to learn and grow
- I allow myself to have fun and be as curious about life again as my child
- I allow myself to learn from my child
- My efforts as a parent are good enough. Who I am is good enough
- I give myself permission to take time out for myself
- I am allowed to rest and take breaks
- I am worth asking for support when I need it
- I can easily make changes when change is immediately needed in my life
- I trust my judgment as a parent

- I am not my mother or my father; I am a unique parent, and my efforts are good enough
- Dinner time is family time with my children
- My children's talents are good enough and they are worthy of praise and love
- My home is a place of peace and healing
- We know how to have fun in our house!

Healing Your Boundaries Finding Peace Again

About the Author

Evette Rose is an Author, Life Coach, Co-Founder of a personal development company and founder of Metaphysical Anatomy. Evette was born in South Africa and grew up in Namibia, West Africa. She then moved to Australia, lived in Vanuatu and Bali. She is best known for her work in helping people to resolve trauma from their past and freeing them to live successful and fulfilling lives. Evette's work is drawn from her own personal experience of moving from a difficult past into a well-balanced life and career. Evette's philosophy is that we, as a human race, are not destined to live our lives in pain due to past trauma or abuse. Humans often suppress their ability to complete or heal trauma naturally. In today's society we often suppress our pain in order to keep up with life and avoid being left behind. Fortunately, through gentle therapy, this natural internal healing instinct can be restored. Writing her books has helped Evette reach out to other people who are in need of love, support, and someone to relate to. She shares her experiences with the world in hopes that it will help people heal and provide encouragement and reassurance when they need it most. Evette now travels the world teaching personal development seminars and continues her research journey. She